HEALTH REPORTS:
DISEASES AND DISORDERS

OBSESSIVE-COMPULSIVE DISORDER

BRUCE M. HYMAN, Ph.D.,
& CHERRY PEDRICK, R.N.

TWENTY-FIRST CENTURY BOOKS
MINNEAPOLIS

Twenty-First Century Books
A division of Lerner Publishing Group, Inc.
241 First Avenue North
Minneapolis, MN 55401 U.S.A.

Website address: www.lernerbooks.com

Library of Congress Cataloging-in-Publication Data

Hyman, Bruce M.
    Obsessive-compulsive disorder / by Bruce M. Hyman, Ph.D, and Cherry
Pedrick, RN.
        p.   cm. — (USA Today Health reports: Diseases and disorders)
    Includes bibliographical references and index.
    ISBN 978-0-7613-5884-8 (lib. bdg. : alk. paper)
    1. Obsessive-compulsive disorder—Juvenile literature. I. Hyman, Bruce M,
Cherry Pedrick. II. Hyman, Bruce M, Cherry Pedrick. Obsessive-compulsive
disorder. I II. Title.
RC533.H948 2011
616.85'227—dc22   2010030787

Manufactured in the United States of America
1 – DP – 12/31/10

CONTENTS

USA TODAY
HEALTH REPORTS:
DISEASES AND DISORDERS

FACES OF OCD

Have you ever wondered if your hands were really clean enough, even after washing them? Have you ever questioned if you locked the door as you walked away from the house? Or maybe if you marked the wrong answer on a test? Or have you ever had bad thoughts, such as really scary, even disgusting and horrible ones that just popped into your mind even though you didn't want to have them? Most people have had these experiences, but they occur as minor, random thoughts or worries that are easily dispelled from their minds. The young people you'll meet in this book have these types of thoughts and worries, but unlike other people, they worry about them most of their waking hours. They have obsessive-compulsive disorder, or OCD, an anxiety disorder marked by persistent, unwanted thoughts that intrude upon the mind, and by compulsive behaviors—unneeded actions that one feels must be done over and over again in certain rigid and consistent ways. You may think you know one of these people, or you might even recognize some of these obsessive-compulsive symptoms in yourself. But these are actual stories of teens who have struggled with OCD.

ANGELA'S STORY

Angela had never cheated on a test. In fact, she was exceptionally honest. In sixth grade, she saw a girl sneak a look at another girl's paper. Their teacher noticed, too, and both girls were sent to the principal's office. The incident bothered Angela and, over the next several days, the scary, unwanted idea of the possibility of her cheating on a test and getting caught began to take up more and more of her thoughts. During the next test, she was consumed by the worry that she might cheat. She thought, What if my eyes wandered and I cheated without my knowing

Some students with OCD worry so much about not cheating on a test that they cannot focus on the test.

it? When she thought it out, it seemed silly and unlikely, but it still distressed her greatly. To counteract the upsetting thought, Angela took extra care to keep her eyes riveted to her paper. She bent down over her desk, just a few inches from her paper, careful not to lift her head or take her eyes off the paper until she was done. Angela complained of back and neck pains after every test. Despite being an excellent student, she had extreme anxiety before and after tests and sometimes stayed home sick on test days.

ALEX'S STORY

Alex also had difficulty taking tests. He studied hard and always knew the material, but he could never finish a test before the time limit was up. He read each question twice before filling in the circles on standardized tests. He felt each circle had to be filled completely, without going outside the lines. His teachers told him that it wasn't necessary to be that meticulous, but he felt compelled to fill the circles completely. After every few questions, he was bombarded by obsessive thoughts that perhaps he filled in the wrong circle. He'd tell himself that he had already checked and he'd been so careful to do it right, but still, he felt compelled to go back and check again. He wound up failing tests.

Like Angela, Alex was a good student, but you'd never know it because he completed only a small part of each test. Homework was a problem too. According to Alex, assignments had to be done perfectly. He erased, rewrote answers, started over, and often gave up without handing in his homework. Alex would stay up late reading, studying, and working on assignments only to "forget" to hand in his work.

NICK'S STORY

In grade school, Nick also had problems with checking. Like Alex, he checked his tests and homework over and over to make certain he'd answered questions properly. He would also check his backpack repeatedly to make sure everything was in its proper place. At home he'd check the stove and appliances to make sure they were turned off when they weren't being used. Sometimes he stood for several minutes flipping the light switch in his room until it felt safe to walk away. He received treatment for obsessive-compulsive disorder, and the checking symptoms improved greatly.

As Nick entered high school, his OCD flared up and took on a different form. Nick and his buddies often teased one another about being or acting gay. However, unlike his friends, who just took it as schoolyard ribbing, Nick became more and more worried by the repetitive thought, What if I really am gay? By all indications, Nick's sexual interests had always been solidly toward the opposite sex. He had never known himself to have even the slightest interest in homosexual relations. However, this idea caused a lightning bolt of fear and doubt in him. He would attempt to block the thought from his mind, but the idea and worry became more intense, consuming him. He wondered, *Why would I even be worried about this? It must mean that I'm gay.*

Nick became more and more conscious of how his friends viewed him. The good-natured ribbing he took from friends fed his increasing doubt and intensified his anxiety and worry. He began to have intrusive and unwanted thoughts of having homosexual relations with men. He also had intrusive thoughts, almost like visions, of walking down the hallway, swinging his arms in a carefree way, and suddenly grabbing another boy's crotch.

To counteract his fears and worries, Nick checked his appearance in the mirror frequently, to make sure he didn't "look gay." He became overly self-conscious about the way he talked to others and walked, vigilantly watching for signs of "being gay." He made sure he didn't hold his arms certain ways, and he averted his eyes from other guys. When he walked down the hallway at school, he kept his hands jammed in his pockets so he wouldn't accidentally touch another boy in a suggestive way. He learned more about OCD on the Internet and e-mailed experts at various OCD websites, asking numerous questions. Was he gay, or was this yet another manifestation of the OCD he'd thought had gone away? How could he tell? Would the thoughts go away with further treatment for OCD?

AMY'S STORY

Amy hated to get her hands sticky or dirty. As a little girl, art class was especially hard to deal with. She couldn't understand why they had to work with paint, glue, paste, and all the other messy things. After art class, she went to the bathroom to wash her hands, but they never felt clean. After being back in class ten minutes, she'd feel as if her hands were sticky again, and then she'd be off to the bathroom again.

Some people with OCD wash their hands compulsively. Their hands become red and chapped.

As a teenager, Amy's obsessions with cleanliness seemed to worsen. She spent longer periods of time in the shower and was often late for school. Trips from the classroom to the bathroom became longer and more frequent.

NATHAN'S STORY

Nathan washed his hands a great deal, too, but not because of stickiness. His fears were of the invisible germs that threatened to make him sick. AIDS (acquired immunodeficiency syndrome) was his original fear. His parents, teachers, and the news media all said it could only be contracted through sexual contact or exposure to blood. But what if they were wrong? What if HIV (human immunodeficiency virus, which causes AIDS) mutated and became more virulent? This fear subsided, only to be replaced by a fear of anthrax, a disease-causing bacteria. It could be anywhere. Hand washing could help prevent skin contact, but anthrax could also be inhaled. Nathan washed his hands a hundred times a day, changed clothes three times a day, and showered every morning, evening, and the moment he returned home. Nathan's trips out of the house became fewer as he stayed home from school more and more often. He sought out information on the Internet about AIDS, anthrax, and other illnesses. He asked his mother to examine his hands often, fearing the redness and dryness from constant washing was a skin disease.

RITA'S STORY

When her sister was born, Rita became fearful that her sister would be hurt or would stop breathing. She got up several times every night to check on her, to make sure she was still breathing. Because of increasing fear of dropping her, she avoided holding her sister. After school Rita went over the day's events, fearful that she had hurt someone by bumping into him or her or saying the wrong thing. She called friends and even classmates she hardly knew to make sure they were okay. At home Rita begged her mother to place the kitchen knives on the top cupboard. She was afraid to touch knives or even know where they were because of these unwanted, horrible, and intrusive thoughts about stabbing family members.

JASON'S STORY

Jason was also afraid of harm coming to others, not so much by doing something to harm them, but by not doing something to protect them from harm. When he went through doorways, he touched the *right side of the doorway, then the left, and then the top. If he didn't do this, he thought harm could come to a family member. Walking down the street, he avoided cracks in the sidewalk. Stepping on one could cause harm, he thought. Sometimes it was inevitable, though, and the harm could be avoided by retracing his steps until it felt okay. He might have to walk back several steps until he "felt right." He knew all this didn't make sense, but he did it anyway, "just in case."*

LUCY'S STORY

Lucy collected things. She had difficulty giving up toys. Then, as a teenager, she couldn't give up books, old makeup, clothing she'd outgrown, old movie tickets, or even corrected school papers and fast-food wrappers. Her room was jammed full of stuff. When it got so full she couldn't walk through it and the bed was covered, her mother would insist that she clean it. Lucy would fill boxes with stuff to be stored in the garage.

CARLOS'S STORY

Unlike Lucy, Carlos kept his room spotless. He dusted and vacuumed every day and kept everything in its place. Books were arranged according to subject, each one exactly 1 inch (2.5 centimeters) from the edge of the shelf. The hangers in his closet were spaced evenly, shirts on the left and pants on the right. Shoes were lined up neatly on the floor. Drawers were just as neat. Each night he laid out his clothes for the next day, along with his backpack and anything else he would be taking to school. At school he placed a pencil and an eraser at the top of his desk and lined up his notebook on the left side with the edge 1 inch (2.5 cm) from the side of the desk.

www.usatoday.com

Life
SECTION D

January 11, 2000

From the Pages of USA TODAY

Mental misery besieges many
Breaking down barriers of bias

People don't get treated for depression because they don't want to admit they have it. The bias against mental illness is still that strong, says David Satcher, U.S. surgeon general.

"But we can and will change the environment to make it more acceptable to say 'I have a mental illness,' just as it is to say 'I have diabetes,'" he says. "The day will come when families can say 'My child is in treatment for depression or anxiety' and not feel this is something that will isolate them."

Satcher's office recently issued the landmark *Mental Health: A Report of the Surgeon General*, which calls for breaking down the social and financial barriers to treatment. Many who are willing to seek long-term care cannot afford it.

Sufferers will lie about mental illness because they fear they will be denied opportunities in the workplace and other environments, Satcher says. "We are going to change that, to make it comfortable to seek treatment."

People should believe treatment works, he emphasizes. The report's major point, Satcher says, "is that for any given mental illness there now exists a range of treatments. Patients should not give up because of the failure of any one."

—*Karen S. Peterson*

Obsessive-compulsive disorder affects 2.5 percent of the American population, most often developing in childhood, adolescence, or young adulthood. Researchers have found that one-third to one-half of OCD cases identified in adults began during childhood. About 1 percent of children have OCD. The good news is that there is hope and help for people struggling with OCD.

CHAPTER ONE

WHAT IS OCD?

ALEX'S STORY

Even as a little boy, Alex always seemed to be worried about something. The feelings of anxiety and fear would hit him suddenly. Something was wrong, but what? He'd check his toys and books, and finding them all in order would help him feel better. At first the peace would last all day, but soon the worries and fears returned full force after a few hours. Then the peace lasted only a few minutes. The anxiety seemed worse every time it returned. He spent more and more time checking, with less relief.

Alex enjoyed school. He learned easily, and his teachers praised him for his neatness. He colored carefully inside the lines and wrote his letters and numbers with great care. Alex worked hard at school and was a straight-A student. When he entered junior high school, the work became more challenging. He fell behind on his homework, and his grades went from As to Bs and Cs. It wasn't that he couldn't do the work. He just didn't have time to complete it. He'd read a page and then worry that he'd missed something and read it again. Assignments had to be neat, so he'd erase and rewrite answers. He questioned his answers and went over his work repeatedly. Alex stayed up late doing homework and then had trouble getting up in the mornings. If papers weren't perfect, he didn't hand them in. Tests were nightmares. He spent a great deal of time filling in the circles on standardized tests. The correct circles had to be filled in completely without going outside the circles. He kept going back to check his answers so often he rarely finished a test.

Alex's parents discussed his schoolwork with him and his teachers. His homeroom teacher suggested maybe they were putting too much *pressure on him to get good grades. Even Alex knew this wasn't the case. His parents had always encouraged him to do his best, but he never felt pressured by them. If anything, he put too much pressure on himself. He felt a need inside to get things right, to get everything right, and to be certain they were right. Schoolwork wasn't the only thing Alex checked. By his early teens, most of his toys were stored in his closet or given away and video games had taken their place. When he finished playing a game, he examined it to make sure it wasn't damaged. Then he'd put it back in the game player and turn it on and off to make certain it still played. Several times a day, he checked the connections between the TV and the video game player and made certain that none of the cords touched one another. He knew this didn't make sense and that it wasn't necessary, but he still felt compelled to check the connections and cords.*

After checking he'd obsess that while he was checking he had actually loosened the connections or, worse, broken the machine. Sometimes he spent an hour checking the connections, arranging the cords, and turning the machine on and off until "it just felt right." As with the compulsive checking of his homework, Alex knew the worries about his video games were excessive. He was ashamed of his behavior and didn't even tell his parents about his checking compulsions. They assumed he was spending the time playing video games.

Alex's grades continued to drop, his anxiety worsened, and his late nights made him increasingly tired and grumpy in the mornings. His mother shared her concerns with the family doctor, who referred him to a psychologist. The psychologist correctly diagnosed him with OCD and began treatment.

UNDERSTANDING OCD

Alex is one of the millions of people around the world who have obsessive-compulsive disorder, a neurobehavioral disorder in which people have obsessions and/or compulsions that are time consuming, distressing, or interfere with normal routines, relationships with others, or daily functioning. Obsessive-compulsive disorder usually develops before the age of thirty but can begin at any time. About sixty-five percent of people with OCD develop the disorder before the age of twenty-five. Many people keep their symptoms secret, not realizing that they have a diagnosable illness. They don't know that one out of every forty people has OCD. Studies in Canada, Puerto Rico, Germany, South Korea, and New Zealand have revealed similar statistics. The disorder exists in every culture, affecting rich and poor alike. Obsessive-compulsive disorder usually has a gradual onset, but it can begin suddenly following a precipitating event, such as emotional stress at home or school, a move to a new neighborhood, health problems, or increased levels of life responsibilities. Women sometimes experience the onset or worsening of symptoms during pregnancy, after giving birth to a child, or after terminating a pregnancy. It's important to realize that the precipitating event does not cause OCD. For the person who has a predisposition for OCD, the event can hasten the onset.

WHAT ARE OBSESSIONS?

Obsessions are persistent impulses, ideas, images, or thoughts that intrude into a person's mind, causing intense anxiety and distress. The person knows the obsessive thoughts are inappropriate and make little sense, but they are so persistent that they are difficult to ignore. They are not the types of thoughts the person would expect to have. Though the thoughts seem to be out of their control, people with OCD do understand that the obsessive thoughts are the product of their own minds and are not imposed from outside themselves.

Compulsion versus Addiction

The compulsions of OCD do not result in pleasure or gratification. Activities such as taking drugs and overeating are not associated with OCD, since these tend to be pleasure-seeking behaviors.

WHAT ARE COMPULSIONS?

Compulsions are repetitive behaviors or mental acts performed in an effort to diminish the anxiety and distress brought on by the obsessive thoughts. Mental acts can include praying, counting, repeating words silently, and going over events in one's mind. The repetitive behaviors include such things as ordering (putting things in order), repeating actions, checking, cleaning, and hand washing. Often the behaviors or mental acts are done with a vague goal of magically preventing or avoiding a dreaded event, death, or illness. Sometimes the compulsions are connected to the dreaded event, but just as often, they are totally unrelated. For example, a person might count to seven to prevent injury to a loved one.

TYPES OF OCD

People with OCD have obsessions. Almost always, they also have compulsions. Some have obsessive thoughts but don't have any outward compulsions. Mental health professionals used to think they had no compulsions at all, but these people usually have compulsive thoughts that are brought to mind to try to get rid of the obsessions. Obsessions and compulsions come in many different types.

Many people with OCD have obsessions and compulsions from two or more categories below, with perhaps one being the most severe. Sometimes one set of obsessions will improve and another set will seem to worsen.

- **Checking.** People who engage in checking have irrational fears of catastrophes befalling themselves or others as a result of things they do or do not do. They may have compulsions to repeatedly check such things as doors, locks, and household appliances to ward off potential disasters. Many also check homework, test questions, and the health or wellbeing of others. The list of things that can be checked is endless, and the more the person with OCD checks, the longer the list of things to be checked becomes.

- **Washing and cleaning.** People who wash and clean excessively have fears and worries about contamination by dirt, germs, or foreign substances. They ease their obsessive fears by washing their hands, showering, or cleaning their environment. Washing and cleaning relieves the distress temporarily, but the fears come back. With time, more washing and cleaning is needed to bring relief.

- **Ordering and repeating.** Those who engage in ordering might feel compelled to arrange certain items in particular, exact, or "perfect" ways. They may be overly concerned with neat handwriting or keeping books and papers in certain places. Others repeat particular actions, such as counting, repeating words, or tapping until they feel "just right." Obsessive thoughts about harm coming to them or a loved one can lead to frenzied ordering or repeating.

- **Experiencing troubling thoughts.** Those with primarily obsessional OCD are troubled by unwanted, intrusive, horrific thoughts and images of causing danger or harm to others.

Examples include unwanted, violent thoughts to harm loved ones or thoughts about engaging in some type of morally unacceptable behavior, such as an embarrassing sexual act. To ease the distress caused by the obsessive thoughts, many purposefully engage in repetitive thoughts, such as praying, counting, or repeating certain words. They may also mentally review distressing situations to reassure themselves. The compulsive thoughts and mental reviews help at first but soon prove inadequate to relieve the anxiety. Cycles of obsessive and compulsive thoughts take up increasing amounts of time, often reaching almost every waking hour. And despite the power and distress of the thoughts, it is the hallmark of the disorder that the person with OCD never actually acts upon the thoughts.

A person with OCD might feel the need to check a lock multiple times or open a locker a certain way.

• **Scrupulosity.** People with scrupulosity have obsessive thoughts that center on religious or moral issues. Often they engage in compulsive prayer or religious services and may seek constant reassurance about their religious beliefs or the morality of their thoughts and/or actions.

- **Hoarding.** People with hoarding collect things that most people would consider junk or trash. People with the compulsion to hoard things might place some significance in the items they collect, but often they can't explain exactly why they feel compelled to collect what they do.

But haven't we all experienced some of these obsessive thoughts and compulsive behaviors at one time or another? Of course we have. Most students have checked a test paper and then felt a need to check it one more time. Many people feel a need to shower or repeat hand washing with no real need to do so. And most of us have collections that others might consider worthless. For most people, checking, cleaning, ordering, worrying, and collecting are things that

The upstairs bedroom of a woman's house in Tennessee is filled with items like old clothes, bags, and boxes. She is a hoarder. She finds it difficult to throw away items that other people would consider trash.

When Obsessions Are a Problem

When obsessive-compulsive behavior significantly interferes with daily living and with functioning at home and school, and when it causes great distress, OCD could be the problem.

can be done or not done by choice. Sometimes overdoing it a little is bothersome to ourselves or others but no big deal. For people with OCD, these behaviors control the person and interfere with daily living.

WHAT CAUSES OCD?

Researchers are piecing together the puzzle that is OCD. The disorder appears, at least in part, to be genetically inherited. Researchers do not believe that a specific gene causes OCD. The transmission of the disorder from generation to generation probably involves multiple genes that affect the brain in complex ways. Inherited subtle variations in brain structure, neurochemistry, and circuitry can predispose a person to develop OCD. Research shows that a higher rate of OCD occurs among relatives of people with OCD. In addition, people with childhood-onset OCD are more likely to have a blood relative with OCD. Environmental factors can also contribute to the development of OCD. A person who is genetically predisposed to OCD may be more susceptible to developing OCD when exposed to environmental stress factors.

www.usatoday.com

USA TODAY

Life
SECTION D

January 15, 2004

From the Pages of USA TODAY

Obsessive-compulsive disorder; Early intervention helps kids who need treatment before rituals are ingrained

At age 8, Elyse of Rhode Island was staying up half the night to do homework.

It's not that her teachers were piling it on. It's that in Elyse's mind, it had to be perfect.

"All my obsessions were on school," she says. "Am I doing this right? I'd spend hours on homework. If I couldn't get a math problem, I'd start crying."

Elyse has obsessive-compulsive disorder. About one-third of adults with the disorder say their symptoms began in childhood, but effective treatments for children are not widely known, and therapists familiar with OCD in children are rare.

In Elyse's case, her father was alert to the symptoms because he has OCD himself. Her parents took her to a doctor for evaluation, and she began weekly therapy.

Her symptoms abated but recur with major life changes. Upon entering high school, "I felt I had so much work to do, I didn't take time to eat. I was out of

control," says Elyse, 17. "I couldn't do my homework; I was obsessing. It just keeps going round and round in circles. I just felt this unbelievable high level of anxiety."

Her worried parents sought help, and Elyse was hospitalized in the adolescent unit at Bradley Hospital in East Providence [Rhode Island] for three weeks. To explain her absence from school, she told her friends she had mononucleosis [a common flu-like disease among adolescents]. "You get really good at hiding it," she says. "People with OCD don't want to show it."

Bradley is one of a handful of hospitals at the forefront of researching OCD in children. Child psychiatrist Henrietta Leonard and psychologist Jennifer Freeman, co-directors of the Pediatric Anxiety Research Clinic at Bradley/Hasbro Research Center in Providence [Rhode Island], are leading studies on how to treat OCD in young children.

The researchers have developed a form of cognitive behavioral therapy, CBT, that is being used successfully to help children as young as 5.

The family is "the critical component of the treatment," Leonard says, so "essentially we teach the family to deliver the CBT treatment."

Young patients are encouraged, gently and over time, to confront whatever it is that they fear.

A child may have washed her hands 30 times in a day but be terrified of leaving the house without washing them once more. In that case, a parent might remind the child of another time when she didn't wash her hands and nothing bad happened, and suggest waiting a few minutes for the fear to pass away.

Often, medications can help. A recent study by researchers at Duke University [in North Carolina] found that a combination of behavioral therapy and anxiety-reducing drugs is more effective than either approach on its own, says pediatrician Susan Swedo of the National Institute of Mental Health. The medications "allow the child to do internal behavioral therapy and provide stress relief."

But treatment can't begin unless there is a diagnosis. About 15% of children with OCD have a relative who also has it, but "most of it comes out of the blue," Swedo says, and parents may not recognize it.

Early diagnosis is important because therapy is more effective before rituals and obsessions become entrenched, and "there's also a demoralization that comes with having symptoms for a long time."

People with OCD know "what they're experiencing doesn't make any sense," she says. "They are frightened and try to hide it as long as possible. People may spend six or seven hours a day on their rituals, and nobody knows."

Elyse was given help at an early age, but she kept her condition a secret until her sophomore year of high school, when she was assigned to write a personal essay and read it aloud in English class.

"I thought this would be a good time to come out about my OCD," Elyse says. The responses from friends "were all so positive. People said: 'If there's anything I can do,' or 'You were strong to come out about it.'"

Buoyed by that support, Elyse has become an advocate for awareness of OCD in teens and children and is active in the Obsessive-Compulsive Foundation, a national research and support group.

Meanwhile, she's busy at school, where she's an A-student, vice president of the student council and secretary of the student government. She also plays field hockey and runs track. She's looking forward to college next fall.

Her OCD is "not completely gone. It's never gone," she says. "It's cyclical. There's always an event that triggers it. Last year, it was the SATs. That was like the only thing I could think about." Her medication was adjusted for a week, "then the SATs were over, and I was fine. But I know there are still bumps in the road."

—Anita Manning

These include psychological and physical trauma, childhood neglect, abuse, family stress, illness, death, and divorce. Major life transitions such as adolescence, moving out, marriage, parenthood, and retirement can also play a role in causing OCD in a person who is biologically/genetically vulnerable.

The neurotransmitter serotonin appears to play an important role in OCD. Neurotransmitters are like chemical bridges that enable communication from one brain cell to another. Brain-imaging studies have shown abnormalities in several parts of the brain in people

Why the body may 'choke'

Excessive activity in the anterior cingulate gyrus (the middle part of the brain) has been associated with mental blocks and other obsessive behavior, causing people to "think too much."

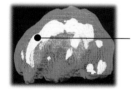

White indicates the most active areas of the brain. In this case it pinpoints overactivity in the anterior cingulate gyrus, the brain's gear shifter.

Cingulate gyrus
Within the frontal lobes

Cerebellum

Healthy image: Shows good, full, symmetrical activity in the front tip of the brain called the prefrontal cortex, the brain's internal monitor or supervisor.

Abnormal image: Identifies decreased activity in the prefrontal cortex, which can cause people to lose focus and have problems with impulse control.

Source: Amen Clinic for Behavioral Medicine, Fairfield, Calif.   By Bob Laird and Frank Pompa, USA TODAY, 2000

with OCD, including the thalamus, basal ganglia, orbital cortex, and cingulate gyrus. These areas of the brain process messages from the outside world, sort information by importance, alert us to danger, and help us focus on the task at hand. In OCD these areas work overtime, focusing on intrusive thoughts and ideas that would normally be filtered out.

PANDAS

Occasionally, children can suddenly develop OCD almost overnight or have a sudden worsening of existing OCD symptoms after they have had strep throat. This reaction to strep is an example of Pediatric Autoimmune Neuropsychiatric Disorders Associated with Streptococcal infections and is often referred to as PANDAS. As many as 25 to 30 percent of childhood-onset OCD cases may be PANDAS related.

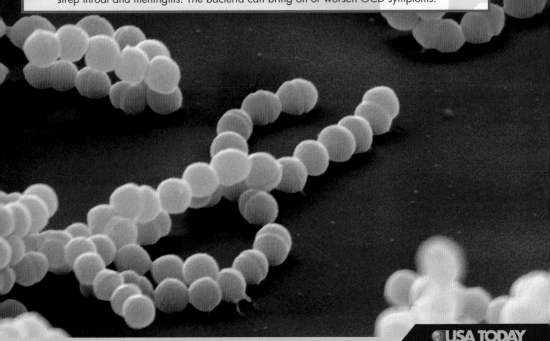

Streptococci bacteria is seen through an electron microscope. This bacteria can cause strep throat and meningitis. The bacteria can bring on or worsen OCD symptoms.

USA TODAY

www.usatoday.com

USA TODAY

Life

SECTION D

January 15, 2004

From the Pages of USA TODAY

Obsessive-compulsive disorder; Early intervention helps kids who need treatment before rituals are ingrained

[P]ediatrician Susan Anderson Swedo of the National Institute of Mental Health] says there is a form of OCD that is associated with a strep infection that affects about one in 10 children with OCD. Called PANDAS (Pediatric Autoimmune Neuropsychiatric Disorders Associated with Streptococcal infections), it is marked by sudden onset of symptoms. "Most OCD starts gradually," Swedo says, but with PANDAS, it can develop in hours. If treated promptly with antibiotics, she says, symptoms can in many cases disappear in days.

—Anita Manning

The body seems to form antibodies against the streptococci bacteria. These antibodies attack the basal ganglia, a key area in the brain, leading to OCD symptoms or worsening of existing symptoms. These develop several months after the strep infection appears to have resolved; onset is sudden and severe. Often other neuropsychiatric symptoms also surface or get worse when the OCD symptoms begin. These can include tics, hyperactivity, handwriting changes, heightened sensory sensitivity, irritability, mood changes, loss of math skills, fidgeting, impulsivity, poor attention span, and separation anxiety.

The Human Brain

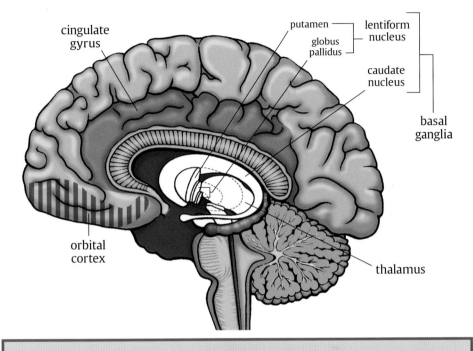

cingulate gyrus

putamen
globus pallidus

lentiform nucleus

caudate nucleus

basal ganglia

orbital cortex

thalamus

> Although researchers do not yet know all the causes of OCD, they do know that in people with OCD, certain parts of the brain work overtime. Studies have shown abnormalities in the thalamus, basal ganglia (which is made up of the caudate nucleus, lentiform nucleus, and other clusters of nerve cells in the deep brain), orbital cortex, and cingulate gyrus of people with OCD.

Detection and treatment of strep infections with antibiotics is essential to the prevention and treatment of PANDAS. Since OCD symptoms often worsen with subsequent strep infections, prompt treatment of strep infections is especially important in susceptible children. Although OCD symptoms improve with antibiotic treatment, some symptoms usually remain and can worsen with time. As with any case of OCD, cognitive-behavioral therapy and/ or medication are often needed to help the child recover.

CHAPTER TWO

THE SYMPTOMS OF OCD

JASON'S STORY

You've probably heard the saying, "Step on a crack, break your mother's back." For Jason and many others, this is more than just a childhood chant, superstition, or game. Their lives are filled with rules. Like most preschoolers, Jason felt more secure when he followed a certain routine. He got upset if bedtime rituals were disturbed. Unlike other children, Jason didn't outgrow his rituals, and over the years, he added more. If things weren't done just right, he had a bad feeling. He couldn't describe it. He just "felt bad." Trying to identify the reason for his uneasiness and anxiety, he spent a lot of time thinking about his feelings. Jason was afraid that something bad would happen to his family or friends. He began to realize his biggest fear was that harm would come to someone he loved and that it would be his fault.

One day Jason walked into a room, bumping the left side of the doorway. He was struck by a fear that something horrible would happen to his mother. He had to do something, anything, to prevent it. He stopped and went back through the doorway. This time he touched the right and then the left side of the doorway. It felt more even, but still, he felt uneasy. He went through again, touching the right, then the left, and then the top. Finally, he felt "okay." The uneasiness was gone, and the fear about harm befalling his mother left him. A few days later, walking into his classroom, Jason was again struck by fear and anxiety. This time he knew how to relieve it. He pretended he had forgotten his pencil and went back to his desk. Then, on the way out, he touched the doorway: right, left, and top. To prevent further episodes, he developed the habit of doing this when he passed through every *doorway. Sometimes it still didn't feel right and he went back through the entrance again.*

With time, he added more rituals. He avoided stepping on cracks on sidewalks and floors. Numbers took on magical qualities—11:11 and 12:12 were especially lucky times of the day. Just noticing these times on his digital watch made for a lucky day. He heated leftovers in the microwave one minute and twenty-three seconds (1–2–3) or two minutes and thirty-four seconds (2–3–4). At first this was just fun, but then it became something he "just had to do."

When Jason was bored, he counted. When he was struck by fear or anxiety (which was becoming more and more often), he counted. He counted the squares in the ceiling, the blinds at the window, his steps, and the number of people in the room. Riding in the car, he counted the telephone poles as the car passed. He became distracted when he listened or read because he counted words in sentences. What would happen if he didn't count the words? Harm to others or to himself? Disaster? Jason wasn't sure. It was all very vague. In reality, he knew it made no sense. All this touching and counting didn't really prevent harm, but it made him feel as if it did. And here was the bigger problem: He was no longer really feeling better. He was counting and touching more and more with less relief.

People like Jason tend to feel as if no one else in the whole world has rituals like theirs. A look at history, though, will find a few very famous and productive people who had OCD and other neurobiological disorders. The eighteenth-century British literary scholar and biographer Samuel Johnson almost certainly had OCD. His biographer James Boswell wrote:

It appeared to me some superstitious habit, which he had contracted early, and from which he had never called upon his

In the 1700s, Samuel Johnson wrote a comprehensive dictionary of the English language. He also displayed symptoms of OCD.

reason to disentangle him. This was his anxious care to go out or in at a door or passage by a certain number of steps from a certain point, or at least so as that either his right or his left foot (I am not certain which) should constantly make the first actual movement when he came close to the door or passage. Thus I conjecture: for I have, upon innumerable occasions, observed him suddenly stop, and then seem to count his steps with a deep earnestness; and when he had neglected or gone wrong in this sort of magical movement, I have seen him go back again, put himself in a proper posture to begin the ceremony, and having gone through it, break from his abstraction, walk briskly on, and join his companion.

Johnson's Accomplishments

I n addition to OCD, Johnson also had symptoms of Tourette's syndrome and depression. Despite these ailments, he wrote the first dictionary of the English language, spending nine years defining more than 40,000 words illustrated with about 114,000 quotations.

DIAGNOSTIC CRITERIA FOR OCD

Mental health professionals rely on the *DSM-IV-TR* (*Diagnostic and Statistical Manual of Mental Disorders*, 4th ed., text revision, 2000) to diagnose mental illness, including neurobehavioral disorders such as OCD. It states:

> The essential features of obsessive-compulsive disorder are recurrent obsessions or compulsions . . . that are severe enough to be time-consuming (i.e., they take more than one hour a day) or cause marked distress or significant impairment. . . . At some point during the course of the disorder, the person has recognized that the obsessions or compulsions are excessive or unreasonable.

Having obsessive thoughts or engaging in compulsive behavior doesn't mean you have OCD. Everyone has occasional intrusive thoughts that are sometimes difficult to get rid of. Most people like to do some things in certain ways, and many people have superstitions. So when does it become OCD? From the criteria we listed, we can ask the following questions. (Answering yes to any of them still doesn't mean a person has OCD. It only means the person should see a qualified mental health professional to check it out.)

- Do you have obsessions and/or compulsions that are severe enough to take up more than one hour a day?
- Do you have obsessions and/or compulsions that cause marked distress—anxiety, fear, apprehension, and dread?
- Do you have obsessions and/or compulsions that cause significant impairment? Do they greatly interfere with your functioning at home, school, or work?
- Do you recognize that your obsessions and/or compulsions seem excessive or unreasonable, even to you?

SYMPTOMS OF OCD

As we've seen, the symptoms of OCD are obsessions and compulsions that take large amounts of time and cause distress. These range from the more common compulsions of washing and checking to less well known symptoms such as hoarding and scrupulosity. Some people will have just one symptom that will always be a challenge, but many will have multiple symptoms. For example, someone who has a problem with checking might also have some problems with washing compulsions.

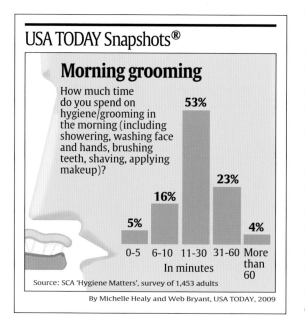

USA TODAY Snapshots®

Morning grooming

How much time do you spend on hygiene/grooming in the morning (including showering, washing face and hands, brushing teeth, shaving, applying makeup)?

- 0-5: 5%
- 6-10: 16%
- 11-30: 53%
- 31-60: 23%
- More than 60: 4%

In minutes

Source: SCA 'Hygiene Matters', survey of 1,453 adults

By Michelle Healy and Web Bryant, USA TODAY, 2009

Symptoms can also change throughout a person's life. Someone who has washing compulsions as a teenager can gain improvement in that set of symptoms, have problems with checking as an adult, and then have intrusive thoughts later in life. Almost everyone could have some of the characteristics associated with OCD at some point, perhaps while stressed, nervous, scared, intimidated, or worried. When these behaviors occur frequently and significantly interfere in everyday life, OCD could be the problem.

SIGNS OF OBSESSIVE-COMPULSIVE DISORDER

- Having excessive concern with dirt and germs
- Frequent hand washing, showering, or grooming, often in a ritualistic manner
- Having red, chapped hands from excessive washing
- Taking long, frequent trips to the bathroom
- Avoiding getting dirty or sticky
- Having chronically untied shoes, since they may be "contaminated"
- Avoiding touching certain things that are believed to be unclean
- Being excessively concerned with bodily secretions and wastes
- Arranging things in a certain order and getting angry or anxious if they are disturbed
- Counting or repeating things a certain number of times
- Considering some numbers "safe" or "bad"
- Repeating rituals such as touching certain things a fixed number of times or going in and out of doors a certain way, for example
- Excessive checking of household things such as doors, lights, locks, windows, or personal items such as toys, music equipment, and homework
- Writing and erasing letters and numbers until they are "just right"

Some people with OCD get easily upset over little things, like not getting called on in class after raising their hand.

- Having excessive fear of harm coming to self or others
- Having unreasonable fear of doing wrong or having done wrong
- Excessive collecting, sometimes of seemingly useless items
- Staying home from school and avoiding usual activities and friends
- Having severe anxiety if usual routines are disrupted
- Daydreaming—which might actually be obsessing, counting, or having other compulsive thoughts.
- Getting upset over minor issues

www.usatoday.com

Life
SECTION D

February 19, 2004

From the Pages of USA TODAY

Animal hoarding: Far beyond 'eccentric'

Dead cats in the yard. A corner knee-deep in animal waste. A stench noticeable three doors down. Andrew Sanderson has seen and smelled it all.

Animal hoarders appear to be a breed apart, possibly with a more serious kind of hoarding. They harbor dozens—sometimes hundreds—of diseased and malnourished animals.

"They think these animals give them unconditional love," says Sanderson, head of animal services in Fairfax County, Va. "They get home from work and the animals rush to them."

It's not love—it's hunger. There's not always enough food to go around. Sanderson has seen plenty of starving animals, elbowed aside by their bigger, stronger housemates.

Some hoarders insist they are running animal-rescue missions, even as they are surrounded by sick animals kept in squa-lor, says veterinarian Gary Patronek, who seven years ago founded the Hoarding of Animals Research Consortium at the Tufts University School of Veterinary Medicine [in Massachussetts].

Animal hoarders tend to be female, elderly and living alone, and cats seem to predominate. A typical case involves 100 to 200 cats, says Randall Lockwood of the Humane Society of the United States.

Up to 2,000 cases of animal hoarding are uncovered in the USA each year, but Lockwood suspects at least as many more hidden cases. Animal-welfare experts struggle to have the condition taken seriously as an illness.

"A lot of these people are still being dismissed as harmless eccentrics," Lockwood says. "If there's a dead animal on the dining- room table, that's not just a lifestyle choice."

—*Joyce Cohen*

- Continuously asking for reassurance about having said or done something wrong
- Asking frequent questions, sometimes rephrasing the same question over and over

www.usatoday.com

USA TODAY

Life

SECTION D

February 19, 2004

From the Pages of USA TODAY

The danger of hoarding; Not only is it a physical threat; it can be a mental problem as well

For 25 years, a problem with a neighbor plagued Curtis and Elaine Colvin of Seattle [Washington]. The neighbor's home and lawn resembled a junkyard.

Finally, last spring, the elderly man was taken out of state by relatives. Konstantinos Apostolou bought the house—and sent in five men to clear the floor-to-ceiling junk.

There was nowhere to walk, except for a narrow "goat path" connecting the rooms. The men hauled out seven dumpsters of clothes, books, magazines, spoiled food, firewood, car parts, tires, bank statements and 50-year-old tax records. "I feel bad for the guy," Apostolou says. "I'm sure he was ill."

Just how ill is still little understood. The man was a classic hoarder—a condition usually considered freakish and laughable or dismissed with cutesy terms like "pack rat" and "junkaholic." Only now is hoarding garnering serious attention.

Hoarders don't just save stuff but constantly acquire new stuff—to such a remarkable degree that it interferes with functioning and safety.

It's unclear how widespread hoarding is, because the problem often surfaces only after a neighbor's complaint or a medical emergency. Randy Frost, a psychology professor at Smith College in Northampton, Mass., estimates that 2% to 3% of the [U.S.] population has OCD, and up to one-third of those exhibit hoarding behavior.

Real danger can lurk in homes overflowing with stuff. Floors buckle from the weight. People get buried under piles. Insects and rodents feast on rotting food. [Items catch on fire], endangering both occupants and firefighters.

Behavioral peculiarities among hoarders come as no surprise to researchers.

For example: "They have rambling or overinclusive speech, where you ask them a question and they tell you a whole story with every possible detail before they get to the answer," says Sanjaya Saxena, a professor at UCLA's [University of California-Los Angeles] School of Medicine.

They have high levels of anxiety, depression and perfectionism. They are greatly indecisive—over what to eat, what to wear. They prepare for all contingencies, keeping items "just in case."

But the true hallmark: "They apply emotions to a range of things that others would consider worthless," Frost says. Where most people see an empty roll of toilet paper, they see art supplies.

At the same time, they tend to be articulate and well-educated, with sophisticated reasons for their saving and acquiring. What if they forgo a newspaper and with it the bit of knowledge that will change their life for the better?

Though people with OCD—those who endlessly wash their hands or check the stove—acknowledge their behavior and are distressed by it, hoarders deny they have a problem.

Brain scans show a difference in brain abnormalities between people with non-hoarding OCD and hoarding OCD, says Saxena of UCLA, who is studying the neurobiology of hoarding.

Whereas non-hoarders show elevated brain activity in certain areas, hoarders show decreased activity in the anterior cingulate gyrus, which deals with focus, attention and decision-making.

Frost suspects there are three categories of hoarders—ordinary hoarders, animal hoarders and trash hoarders. The latter two seem much more severe, he says. But the dividing lines are murky and overlapping.

Almost always, if a place is cleaned out, the hoarding behavior returns immediately.

In Pittsfield, Mass., fire chief Stephen Duffy tells of one elderly widow whose house had "debris piled higher than the bed, with one spot where she curled up on the mattress to sleep."

The woman was relocated to an assisted-living complex, Duffy says. She immediately "returned to the house, packed garbage bags full of things, and brought them back" to the assisted-living home.

—Joyce Cohen

A crew of movers haul boxes of items from a hoarder's home. The amount of material in the home posed a danger to the family living there.

WHAT OCD IS NOT

An important part of understanding OCD is understanding what OCD is not. We've already discussed how the obsessions and compulsions have to be excessive and have to significantly interfere with life. Even when this is the case, sometimes the problem may not be OCD.

NORMAL CHILDHOOD DEVELOPMENT

Most young children exhibit compulsive or ritualistic behaviors to help them control their environment and to master childhood fears and anxieties. Bedtime rituals, collecting things, superstitions, and rigid adherence to rules of games are examples of the regular compulsions of childhood. When they can't engage in the compulsive behavior, children can become anxious and angry. They give up most of these behaviors by the time they reach nine or ten years old. As children mature and move into adolescence, they loosen up a bit. Devotion to activities and sports is common, collecting and rules are still important, but the rigidity lessens. Breaking the rules and missing out on an important addition to a collection can cause distress, but it's more easily dealt with.

Compulsive behaviors of OCD in children go beyond developmental rituals. The child gains some pleasure and comfort at first, but it's fleeting. Anxiety returns full force, requiring more and more rituals. The behavior is excessive and may not make any sense at all. Though younger children may believe their rituals are necessary, most older children and teens know that the behavior is excessive.

SUPERSTITIONS, RITUALS, PRAYERS , AND WORRY

Superstitions, customs, rituals, and prayers are part of everyday life. When these are done for cultural or religious reasons, they are not

Extreme nervousness can take over the life of a person with OCD. Other disorders can cause this feeling, too, and should be looked into to determine the cause.

OCD. If the behaviors take over one's life, causing significant distress and anxiety, or are quite time consuming, OCD could be the problem. What about worry? We all worry at times, but when worry is excessive, irrational, or causes a lot of anxiety, it needs to be looked into. If it isn't OCD, it could be a symptom of depression or another anxiety disorder.

SUBSTANCE ABUSE AND PATHOLOGICAL GAMBLING

Pathological gambling and addiction to substances such as drugs or alcohol are called impulse control disorders. Unlike OCD, they involve engaging in behaviors that bring about instantaneous pleasure.

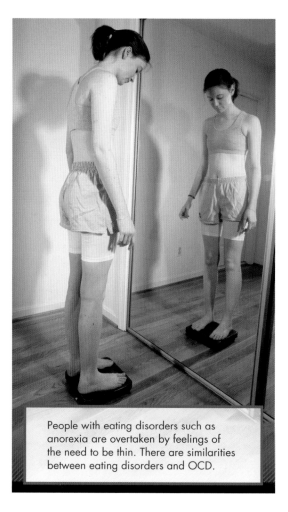

People with eating disorders such as anorexia are overtaken by feelings of the need to be thin. There are similarities between eating disorders and OCD.

OCD, in contrast, involves engaging in behaviors that are meant to reduce distress. Because the reasons for the behaviors differ, the treatments of the disorders differ.

EATING DISORDERS

Similarities exist between OCD and the over-preoccupation with food and thinness found in such disorders as compulsive eating, anorexia nervosa, and bulimia. Some people with eating disorders have obsessive-compulsive symptoms and can benefit from the treatment strategies used to treat OCD. Eating disorders can be quite serious, even life threatening, so it's very important to seek professional help if one is suspected.

OBSESSIVE-COMPULSIVE PERSONALITY DISORDER

Have you ever been called a control freak? Do you get caught up in the details of projects and assignments to the point where you get little or nothing done? Do you make endless lists of things you have to do but then never even look at them? Do you have trouble making even simple decisions for fear of making a mistake? Does everything you do take extra time because it must all be done "perfectly"? Are you a person who must have everything your way and believes your way is the only "right" way? You've probably met people like this in your life at some time or another. These behaviors constitute the features of obsessive-compulsive personality.

Many of the features of obsessive-compulsive personality are valued in our culture (you would probably want your heart surgeon to have features of obsessive-compulsive personality). But while many people have moderate features of obsessive-compulsive personality, in a minority of instances, the behaviors seriously interfere with a person's relationships at work and home. In this instance, it is referred to as obsessive-compulsive personality disorder, or OCPD.

When we think of a personality, we generally use phrases such as: "She has a nice, caring personality" or "He has a strong, domineering personality." A personality is a lifelong, consistent set of learned and inherited responses to a wide range of situations in life. These characteristics don't change too much throughout the life span and are what make each of us unique or different.

When a particular "style" or set of features of a personality causes an excess of distress or difficulty in life, a person is said to have a personality disorder. According to the *DSM-IV-TR*, people with obsessive-compulsive personality disorder are characterized by an excessive concern with details, rules, lists, orderliness, perfectionism, and being in control. These traits contrast with seeing the "big picture" and being flexible, open to others, and efficient. People with OCPD tend to view the world in "black-and-white, all-or-nothing" terms. For them, there are no gray areas in life.

As workers they tend to be highly efficient, reliable, and organized—but often to excess. They may get over-involved with the details of a task, often "not seeing the forest for the trees," thereby getting way behind or even not completing the task at all. In their personal life, they spurn change and spontaneity, instead preferring predictability, repetition, and a highly routine way of life. They tend to keep their emotions and behavior very controlled, appearing rather cold and aloof to others.

People with OCPD are inclined to think quite highly of themselves, tending to blame the problems of life on others, rather than on their own flaws, shortcomings, and failings. Any suggestion of personal responsibility for problems is likely to be met with great resistance. As a result, they are reluctant to accept guidance and intervention from outside themselves, which might imply they are less than "perfect."

Occasionally a person with OCPD also has OCD. The perfectionism, rigidity, and need for control make treatment more difficult. People with OCPD have difficulty accepting guidance and intervention from others because this would mean that they are less than "perfect." When they finally do realize they need help and seek out a professional, they may have lost everything. However, with persistence and determination, even people with OCPD can, with help, make meaningful changes in their approach to living that can open the door to a better quality of life.

OCD vs. OCPD

While the characteristics of OCPD tend to be pretty consistent through a person's life, the symptoms of OCD tend to rise and fall through life. People with OCD suffer substantially from their problem and wish to be rid of it. OCD can be helped significantly with medication and cognitive-behavioral therapy. On the other hand, people with OCPD do not change from the use of medication. While they may be helped with long-term "talk" psychotherapy, they don't usually change until they "hit bottom"—suffering substantial losses in their work and personal lives.

CHAPTER THREE

TREATMENT OF OCD

AMY'S STORY

Amy couldn't explain why, but she just didn't like to get her hands dirty or sticky. She dreaded working with paint, glue, and paste in art class and avoided other activities that meant getting her hands sticky. She stayed inside whenever she could so she wouldn't get dirty. When she did get her hands dirty, she washed them well. Most people would say too well. She counted to twenty when she washed her hands because she had learned it took twenty seconds to clean your hands really well. But sometimes that didn't seem long enough. They just did not seem clean, so she washed them longer, until it "felt right." After drying her hands, she'd head for the door, then be struck by the thought that they still weren't clean enough, and start the process all over again. After art class, lunch, and snacks, or whenever Amy felt her hands were dirty, she raised her hand to go to the bathroom. Occasionally, her teachers got suspicious and wondered why she was making so many trips to the bathroom. She made excuses and sometimes complained of feeling ill so she could go home. Amy often did feel sick. She was so worried about her hands being dirty and sticky that she felt anxious and sick all over. Her stomach would hurt, and she felt as if her heart was racing. What if they were dirty? What if hidden germs were on her hands? She could get sick or pass germs onto someone else and therefore be held responsible for getting others sick too.

At home Amy's worries about cleanliness went beyond her hands. To protect her family members, she changed her clothes and shoes as soon as she got home from school and removed them immediately from her room. She asked the rest of the family to do the same. The laundry basket and the family's shoes had to stay in the utility room, far from the bedrooms. Amy insisted on long baths at night and then spent at least an hour getting ready for bed. She spent a lot of time brushing her teeth and repeatedly asked her mother for reassurance that they were clean enough. She never wore anything but "perfectly" clean pajamas each night.

Amy's obsessions with cleanliness only worsened as she became a teenager. Her showers lasted longer and longer, almost an hour, and one per day was never enough. She washed her body in a specific order, each body part five times. Her face took the longest, as she worried a great deal about the onset of acne. Amy was late for the school bus most days, so her mother drove her to school. This was just as well anyway because she felt the bus was "contaminated." The floor was filthy, and the seats were dirty and sticky.

At school Amy's trips to the bathroom became more frequent and prolonged. She withdrew from her friends, afraid to get too close to most people because touching others meant several minutes of hand washing. While she tried to keep it a closely held secret, her friends often noticed Amy's discomfort around them. She seemed to be "dazed out," as her mind was filled with constant fear and worry. Many days she just stayed home sick from school. Her mother considered home schooling as a last resort.

HOW IS OCD DIAGNOSED?

Long ago, obsessive-compulsive disorder was considered such a severe mental illness that most mental health professionals thought it to be untreatable. All mental illnesses carried a stigma. But thanks to decades of research into the neurophysiology of OCD, researchers have developed effective treatments for OCD. As a result, this mental illness is losing the stigma it once had. Through informative media coverage and greater openness, the public is becoming educated to the idea that most mental illnesses, including OCD, are caused by the same types of "physical" factors as other so-called physical diseases.

The average person doesn't seek treatment for OCD until seven to ten years after the first symptoms of OCD show up. This waiting time can make a difference in the course of the illness. With time, the obsessive thoughts and compulsive behaviors become more ingrained, more a part of the person's daily life, thus harder to successfully treat.

The sooner help is sought, the earlier in life the symptoms can be controlled and the sooner the person can be on the road to recovery. The first step toward recovery is diagnosis. Obsessive-compulsive disorder is diagnosed on the basis of a psychiatric examination by a qualified mental health professional, preferably a psychiatrist or psychologist who specializes in the treatment of OCD. An interview is the most important part of the process, but some valuable questionnaires are also used to arrive at a diagnosis. A medical exam may also be ordered to rule out other health problems.

How does one find a mental health professional who is qualified to diagnose OCD or another anxiety disorder? Most people will begin with an appointment with their family doctor or perhaps a school counselor. While some counselors and physicians may not be familiar with OCD, they are usually trained to pick up on the signs of depression and anxiety that often go along with OCD.

Sometimes people are hesitant to share their symptoms, even with their doctor. This is the irony of OCD. People with OCD usually know their compulsive behaviors are excessive and unneeded, but feel a need to do them anyway. They might be ashamed of what they feel are ridiculous behaviors and be embarrassed that they can't "just stop." Getting help takes courage. Almost always, though, the fears linked to reaching out are unfounded. Instead of ridicule, most people find understanding and compassion. Sharing information about obsessive-compulsive symptoms with a school counselor or family doctor can be an important first step toward obtaining the help needed to battle OCD.

TREATMENT OPTIONS

Effective treatments for OCD are available. There is no known cure for OCD, but two treatments have been proven effective in making the symptoms manageable. Medications have been developed that can ease the symptoms of OCD. Cognitive-behavioral therapy (CBT) is used to help change the behavior and thought patterns of OCD. Often, medication is combined with therapy. The right treatment can help a person with OCD live a satisfying, productive life. Without treatment, life can be filled with needless, severe anxiety and distress.

MEDICATION

Antidepressants, a group of medications used to treat depression, have been found to be highly effective in the treatment of OCD. These medications are from a family of medications called selective serotonin reuptake inhibitors, or SSRIs. They include fluvoxamine (Luvox), fluoxetine (Prozac), sertraline (Zoloft), paroxetine (Paxil), citalopram (Celexa), and escitalopram (Lexapro). They work by increasing the amount of serotonin available to the nerve cells in the brain. Venlafaxine (Effexor), duloxetine (Cymbalta), and other antidepressants may also be useful, however more study is needed.

Anafranil is an older tricyclic antidepressant that was considered the first breakthrough drug for the treatment of OCD when it came out in the 1980s. It is still used to treat OCD. It has an effect on both serotonin and other neurotransmitters.

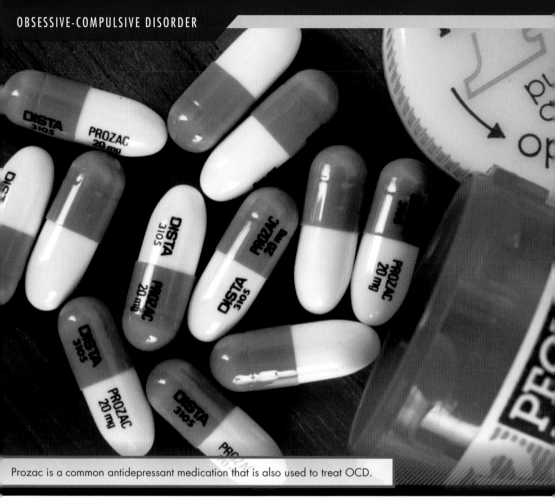

Prozac is a common antidepressant medication that is also used to treat OCD.

Neurotransmitters are brain chemicals that enable messages to be carried back and forth between nerve cells. They are vital to our brain's capacity to properly regulate our moods. In people with OCD, serotonin is not being properly regulated in the brain. Imbalances of serotonin and other chemicals contribute to OCD symptoms. For reasons that are not completely understood, SSRI medications correct these imbalances, thereby reducing the symptoms of OCD in most patients.

Medication is often an important part of the treatment of OCD. It can reduce the intensity of obsessive thoughts and the urge to engage in rituals. These medications work in very similar ways to relieve obsessive-compulsive symptoms, but each is somewhat different.

Each has a slightly different effect upon nerve cells that differs from person to person. As a result, a medication, such as Prozac, for example, that works very well for one patient with OCD may have no effect upon another. Therefore, at times, several medications must be tried before the one is found that works best for an individual.

Usually, a positive response is seen within six to eight weeks. However, patience is vital, as it can take twelve weeks or even longer to find out if a medication is going to be effective. Fortunately, if one medication doesn't work, doctors have several other potentially effective ones to choose from. One will be discontinued and another started. Sometimes other medications must be added to SSRIs to get relief of OCD symptoms and the anxiety it causes.

Once the person with OCD shows a positive response to a medication, it's important to stay on the medication at what is called a maintenance dose. This is the least amount of medication necessary to keep the symptoms under good control. Studies have shown that the majority of patients who are not receiving cognitive-behavioral therapy (80 to 90 percent or more) will relapse upon discontinuation of the medication.

Only rarely does medication alone result in the complete elimination of OCD symptoms. More typically the patient, while improved, may still have some bothersome symptoms. For the most effective lifelong management of OCD, it's best to obtain treatment with cognitive-behavioral therapy.

COGNITIVE-BEHAVIORAL THERAPY

Cognitive-behavioral therapy has been shown to be highly beneficial in the treatment of OCD. This is actually the combination of two treatment approaches, cognitive therapy and behavior therapy. The "cognitive" in cognitive-behavioral therapy refers to strategies that

Medication and CBT

For patients taking medications for OCD, the addition of cognitive-behavioral therapy has a number of benefits. Aside from improving the severity of symptoms, studies have shown that patients successfully treated with cognitive-behavioral therapy are more likely to do well should medications be discontinued or the dosage reduced.

help people change dysfunctional thinking patterns and beliefs. One example of a dysfunctional thinking pattern in OCD patients is "overvaluation of thought." This refers to the tendency in OCD to give thoughts, especially scary or disturbing thoughts, too much meaning and importance. Cognitive therapy helps a person alter this troublesome thinking pattern to more appropriate ones.

While often very helpful, cognitive therapy has its limitations. After all, people with OCD have already tried, endlessly, to talk themselves out of their obsessive thoughts and compulsive behaviors. The behavioral part of cognitive-behavioral therapy refers to using exposure and response prevention (ERP) to alter compulsive behaviors such as washing and checking. Combining the cognitive and behavioral parts of cognitive-behavioral therapy provides powerful tools to manage obsessive-compulsive symptoms. People with OCD can then lead more productive lives. Let's look at one of the key components of CBT for OCD.

EXPOSURE AND RESPONSE PREVENTION

The technique considered to be "the gold standard" in the treatment of OCD is exposure and response prevention, also called exposure and ritual prevention. This is because numerous scientific studies, as well as the reports of thousands of patients who have been successfully treated with it, have shown it to be effective in reducing OCD symptoms.

Just what happens in exposure and response prevention? Exposure involves placing yourself in the very situation that provokes fear and dread. Exposure reduces the anxiety and distress of fear-provoking situations through habituation. Here's how it works: Our nervous system naturally goes through this process whenever we "get used to" something that at first jolts us or causes fear. A good example is seeing a really scary horror movie. The first time you see it, you are surprised, shocked, even grossed out. You decide to see it again, but this time the movie doesn't seem so scary. The shocking parts become predictable, and the gross parts become not so gross anymore. You decide to sit through it a third time, and it's utterly boring. The prolonged repetition of the same movie has caused your nervous system to go "Ho hum, I've seen this before." This is like the process of nervous system habituation.

Another example is easing yourself into a swimming pool filled with cold water. Imagine sitting on the edge of a pool and dipping your foot into the cold water. At first it feels uncomfortably frigid. You want to immediately pull your foot out. But if you keep your foot in the water, after about thirty seconds something changes. It feels comfortable on your foot. What changed? Did the water temperature change? Of course not. After prolonged exposure to the cold water, the temperature sensory neurons in your skin "got used to" or "habituated to" the sensations of the cold water.

The technique of exposure uses this natural process of habituation to help people overcome irrational fears (called phobias) of all types. Imagine, for example, that you never learned to swim and, as a result, you're fearful or terrified of the water. The very thought of getting within a few feet of a swimming pool is terrifying. Through the process of exposure, your fear can be overcome. First, you walk within a few feet of the swimming pool. You feel immediate

By slowly exposing oneself to one's fears (such as the fear of water) through exposure and response prevention (ERP), people can often overcome their fears.

discomfort. Your heart races, stomach churns, palms get sweaty, and mouth gets dry. After a few minutes, the initial fear you felt starts to lessen as your nervous system habituates to the idea of being within a few feet of the dreaded swimming pool.

Having conquered being a few feet from the pool, you feel brave, so you inch closer to the pool's edge, and again, your fear rises with accompanying feelings: Your heart races, breathing pace increases, hands get clammy, and you feel "butterflies" in your stomach. You don't move but stay where you are. Again, after time passes, your fear lessens as you habituate to the idea of nearness to the pool. Determined to get into the pool, you place one toe into the water, and once again the fear rises. But as before, after a few minutes, your nervous system habituates to the water. You submerge your ankle, then calf, and then knee. Slowly but gradually, you are in the water up to your waist, thanks to the capacity of your nervous system to adapt to the feared situation through habituation. You have mastered your fear by quieting your brain's natural alarm signals.

Exposure works to help the person with OCD overcome fears in the same way. In ERP, people with OCD are asked to expose themselves to the things they fear, much as in the previous example with the fear of water. The approach is gradual, like moving slowly into the feared swimming pool. The ultimate goal is complete habituation to the feared object or situation. For example, Amy might touch something she considers dirty or contaminated with only the tip of a finger at first and then with several fingers.

Exposure is only half the story in ERP. The other important component is response prevention. This means actively and purposefully not doing whatever the person usually feels compelled to do to relieve the anxiety and distress of the obsessive thoughts, such as hand washing, checking the door locks over and over, counting, or rethinking a thought "correctly." The goal here is to allow natural habituation to lessen the anxiety of the thought, rather than trying to get anxiety relief through the compulsive behavior. It's important to experience a moderate amount of anxiety and continue the exposure long enough for the anxiety to rise and then fall to manageable levels. When habituation occurs, the mind has the chance to "realize" that the feared consequences, such as getting sick or burning the house down, aren't going to happen after all.

When exposure is combined with response prevention, more appropriate reactions to the anxiety-provoking thoughts can be learned, and therefore, great progress can be made toward overcoming OCD. Doing ERP is highly challenging because the person initially feels very anxious as anxiety-producing situations are confronted and learned habits of doing rituals in response to the anxiety are blocked.

Sometimes it may be too difficult to resist doing the ritual. The person with OCD might choose, instead of completely stopping the ritual, to delay it or alter it in small ways, working gradually toward completely stopping. Sometimes it's almost impossible to do real-life ERP, as in the case of the obsession about possibly causing harm to others. Then a related technique called imaginal exposure is done.

In doing imaginal exposure, people with OCD are challenged to think their scariest thoughts by writing a short story that describes their most unthinkable fear in detail. For example, Rita's imaginal exposure story might involve forgetting to check that her sister was breathing. That morning, in the story, her parents find her sister limp in bed, call an ambulance, and then blame Rita for not making sure that her sister was OK and breathing. She then fears that she will be punished forever by her parents, God, and everyone, for her failure. Jason's imaginal exposure story would involve failing to step on sidewalk cracks perfectly, resulting in his mother getting sick.

The Objective of ERP

It's important to make certain that exposure therapy brings up the actual anxious feelings it's designed to help control. The objective is to experience the anxiety and realize that it can be tolerated without doing the usual rituals.

Jason feels extremely guilty and sad forever because he did not do his ritual properly.

After the story is written (usually in first person), it is read over and over for at least forty-five minutes per day. The story can also be recorded on a tape recorder or burned to a CD for repeated listening. The story is read or listened to daily until habituation occurs. Usually, the imaginal exposure exercises help people realize the senselessness of their beliefs and the behaviors needlessly used to cope with their fears. The result is to help people with OCD better tolerate the discomfort of thinking a scary thought.

Treatment with ERP is hard work and requires patience and persistence to be successful. Even after the therapy ends, most people with OCD will need to continue using ERP principles, sometimes for the rest of their lives. Some may even need to return to therapy for "booster sessions" to increase their ERP skills. While ERP principles are described in several self-help books, it's best to get started with a qualified mental health professional who is specifically trained in using ERP with people with OCD. This is especially important for children and teens.

MEDICATION, COGNITIVE BEHAVIORAL THERAPY, OR BOTH?

Which treatment choice is best is a common question asked by patients and family members. The answer is that both cognitive-behavioral therapy and medication play an important role in relieving OCD symptoms. It's best to think of each course of treatment, either medication or CBT, as only partial treatment. Some people with more severe checking and washing symptoms may need to start medication first and gain some initial relief prior to starting CBT. Others may get very little relief from medication, with a few finding the side effects intolerable. Those patients will require CBT to make progress. Most people with OCD, however, will benefit from a combination of medication and CBT. Medication can be likened to the "water wings" kids use when they're learning to swim. As medications reduce anxiety, relieve depression, and improve mood, focus and concentration, they provide the "water wings" sometimes needed when people with OCD are learning CBT techniques to reduce their obsessive thoughts and compulsive rituals.

PSYCHOTHERAPY

Years ago, before research helped us better understand OCD, the disorder was thought to be caused solely by life experiences. Unhappy childhoods, dysfunctional relationships with parents, and learned behaviors such as excessive cleanliness were often blamed. We now know this isn't the case. In traditional psychotherapy, or "talk therapy," patients discuss with a therapist their dissatisfactions about their past that are contributing to their present problems. Traditional psychotherapy does not appear, in itself, to be an effective treatment for OCD. It may, however, be very helpful in conjunction with cognitive-behavioral therapy, especially if the person has life

Talking to a therapist can help some people with OCD deal with the stress they experience in their lives.

problems, such as a strained marriage, illness in the family, or job loss that may be aggravating the OCD. Talking out and expressing pent-up feelings honestly and openly with a trained professional can provide great comfort and relief during difficult times when OCD symptoms threaten to break loose. Talk therapy can also help a person cope with stress. Stress can make OCD symptoms more severe. Focusing on obsessive perfectionism, doubting, procrastination, and indecisiveness can aid in getting the person to use medication and cognitive-behavioral therapy.

Besides the stressers from life problems, OCD itself often creates great strain among family members. Family therapy with a skilled therapist familiar with OCD can help family members address these often sticky issues directly with one another "safely" and objectively.

Acceptance and Commitment Therapy

People can be so consumed with getting rid of their symptoms that they can put their life on hold and actually create another obsession. It's important to stop and get off the fixing treadmill, stop trying, and start living *in spite of* OCD symptoms. Dr. Bruce Hyman describes a new, so-called third-wave therapy designed to help people with OCD do just that in *The OCD Workbook*. It's called acceptance and commitment therapy, or ACT (pronounced as one word, not the individual letters), and it just may be the "next big thing" in the cognitive behavioral treatment of anxiety disorders, including OCD. From the viewpoint of ACT, people can control their compulsions, but not necessarily their obsessions and anxiety. When a person can think of the goal as controlling compulsive behaviors rather than controlling obsessive thoughts and anxiety, the person will see OCD in a whole new way.

Acceptance and commitment therapy was developed in the mid-1980s by Dr. Steven Hayes, a psychology professor at the University of Nevada, Reno, who has since been quietly transforming the ways that mental health professionals think about a whole range of disorders, including OCD. While the ACT approach to helping OCD is consistent with the cognitive behavioral principles underlying exposure and response prevention, it differs in several important ways. ACT doesn't focus on getting rid of painful thoughts, feelings, and experiences, and in fact, it views these as inevitable in life. Instead, it's oriented toward learning how to live more in the present, with more of a focus on your goals and values, while making room for difficult internal experiences. ACT teaches people how to engage with painful thoughts and feelings and how to become more comfortable with them through acceptance and mindfulness. Another important goal of ACT is developing self-compassion and flexibility. All of these aspects are aimed at helping people build life-enhancing patterns of behavior. ACT isn't about overcoming pain or fighting thoughts or emotions; it's about embracing life and experiencing everything it has to offer, both the positive, such as joy, and the challenges, including fear, anxiety, and worry.

ACT offers a way out of suffering by helping you learn how to live the life you most desire while experiencing whatever you experience along the way. ACT has evolved within a solid scientific tradition. A thriving research community is actively engaged in examining the basic science underlying ACT and the effectiveness of applying ACT techniques to numerous life problems, including OCD, anxiety disorders, depression, and substance abuse, just to name a few. The ACT model is based on six core principles that play an important role in behavioral and psychological flexibility. The six core principles are:

Experiential acceptance (versus avoidance)

This means being willing to make room for unpleasant feelings, sensations, and urges, allowing them to come and go without struggling with them, avoiding them, or paying excessive attention to them. The goal isn't necessarily to rid yourself of these thoughts; it's learning to not buy into the content of the thoughts and learning to pursue valued directions in life despite their presence.

Contact with the present moment, or mindfulness

Mindfulness is the practice of consciously bringing awareness to your here-and-now experience, including your thoughts, with openness, interest, and

receptiveness. Through practice in mindfulness, you learn how to allow your thoughts and feelings to be what they are, letting them come and go without buying into them or struggling with them.

Cognitive defusion (versus fusion)

Cognitive fusion refers to the human tendency to get caught up in our thoughts and assume that thinking has as much power as real events in our lives. Cognitive fusion means that you take your thoughts to be all-important, identify with them, and even fear them. In contrast, cognitive defusion means being able to step back from one's thoughts and observe them without being caught up in their content.

Self-as-context, or the observing self

Self-as-context refers to the "you" that is always there observing and experiencing, and that is distinct and separate from your thoughts, feelings, sensations, images, and memories. In ACT, this is sometimes referred to as the observing self or the transcendent self.

Values

In terms of OCD, values can help you redirect your time and energy away from futile and costly goals (trying to control or avoid thoughts, internal images, and sensations), and toward a life that stands for what's important to you. In values work, you're encouraged to actively and specifically

NEUROSURGERY

Most people will get some relief from their OCD symptoms from medication and/or cognitive-behavioral therapy. A very, very small number of people with severe and disabling symptoms define what matters most in your life and the sort of person you want to be.

Committed action

Improvements are made in the person's quality of life by working toward goals: committed actions in the service of the person's values. Symptom reduction per se isn't the goal, but it is often a natural side effect of sustained, committed actions toward one's core values.

In ACT, progress toward treatment goals isn't measured by the degree of symptom reduction you achieve. Rather, your progress is measured by the degree to which you're living your life in alignment with your values, despite the presence of difficult thoughts.

ACT is being evaluated for its effectiveness as a treatment for OCD and other anxiety disorders, and the results are promising. At present, exposure and response prevention is still recommended as the first-line treatment approach for OCD. After doing ERP for about six weeks, a person with OCD may want to utilize some ACT ideas. People with particularly strong avoidance tendencies may find ACT to be especially useful.

aren't helped by these treatments. Neurosurgery can help the most treatment-resistant patients, but it doesn't usually relieve all the symptoms. Cognitive-behavioral therapy and/ or medication are often important postoperative treatments.

USA TODAY

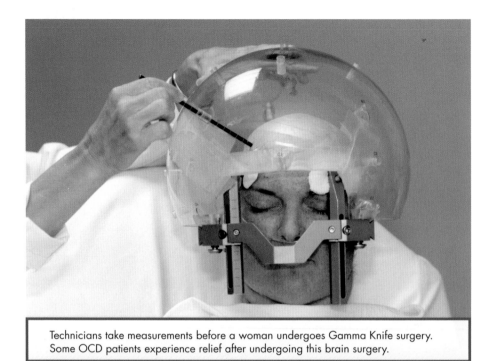

Technicians take measurements before a woman undergoes Gamma Knife surgery. Some OCD patients experience relief after undergoing this brain surgery.

Symptoms usually improve over several weeks or months, rather than immediately.

Since the early 1990s, a surgical tool known as a Gamma Knife has been successfully used to perform noninvasive brain surgery on patients with OCD. The Gamma Knife focuses gamma-ray beams into a single point and creates tiny lesions deep in the brain. The procedure avoids the complications of more invasive surgeries, such as infections, hemorrhage, seizures, and wound healing. Side effects include headaches (about 10 percent of patients) and, rarely, apathy and decreased motivation.

Research is being done on deep brain stimulation, or DBS, for treating OCD. A French neurosurgeon discovered this procedure by accident in 1987 while using an electrical probe in the brain of a patient with Parkinson's disease. When an electrical current accidentally touched a part of the brain called the thalamus, the patient's tremors stopped. DBS is approved in the United States for the treatment of Parkinson's and essential tremor. Studies show some promising results for DBS as a treatment for severe OCD symptoms.

Both the Gamma Knife and DBS treatments attempt to correct what researchers consider higher-than-normal metabolic brain activity in OCD patients. While the Gamma Knife severs connections between affected areas of the brain, the DBS pacemaker uses electrodes to electrically jam the nerve impulses in the connections so their messages are not transmitted. Recovery time is longer for DBS surgery, and some risk of hemorrhage and infection exists. Unlike the Gamma Knife surgery, DBS is reversible. The DBS electrodes can be turned off and the pacemaker can be fine-tuned to find an optimal level of electrical stimulation.

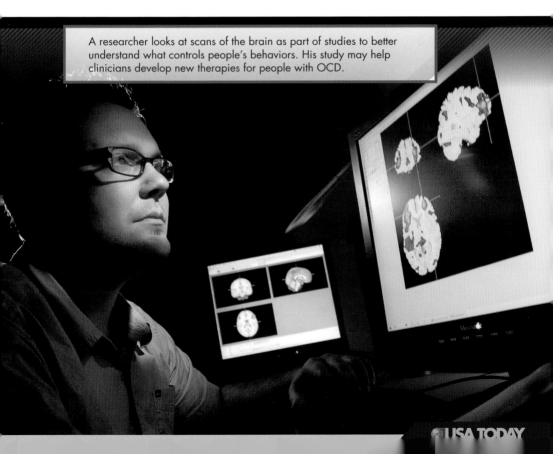

A researcher looks at scans of the brain as part of studies to better understand what controls people's behaviors. His study may help clinicians develop new therapies for people with OCD.

USA TODAY

www.usatoday.com

USA TODAY

Life

SECTION D

February 19, 2004

From the Pages of USA TODAY

Could you be a border hoarder?

Many people see traces of hoarding behavior in themselves. Though having a big mess is a far cry from pathological hoarding, such behavior appears to be on a continuum.

Professionals who run self-help groups for mild or borderline hoarders—those chronic clutterers who acknowledge their problem and are truly motivated to change—offer this advice:

- Excavate one tiny area at a time—one tabletop, one corner, one drawer, one shelf in the medicine cabinet.
- Sort before discarding anything. It's hard to [let go of] one scarf but less hard to get rid of 20 out of 40.
- Wear those unworn clothes. If something feels wrong or you dislike wearing it, consider whether it's worth keeping. Even a reluctance to wear something is telling.
- Donate items instead of throwing them away, because it's a comfort to know they can find a good home with someone else.
- Don't buy a book unless you spend half an hour with it in the bookstore. For every book acquired, [give away] two books you have already identified as dispensable.
- Control acquisition by imagining you must pay a dollar for every "free" thing.
- Take before-and-after photos so you can see the difference and chart your progress.

—Joyce Cohen

RELATED DISORDERS

Some psychiatric disorders appear to be related to OCD. Symptoms such as repetitive and intrusive thoughts play a major part in these disorders. We call these obsessive-compulsive spectrum disorders, or OCSDs. They include trichotillomania (TTM), self-injurious skin picking, body dysmorphic disorder (BDD), and hypochondriasis.

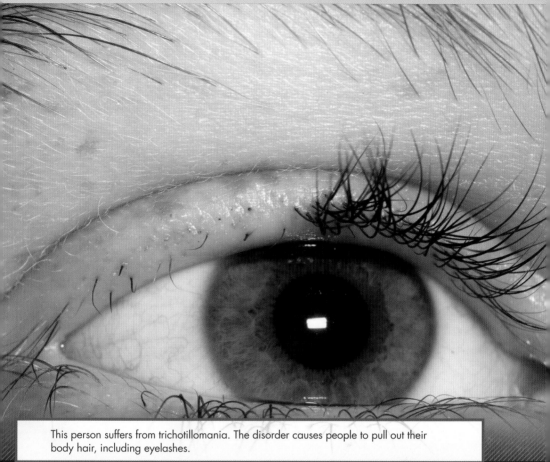

This person suffers from trichotillomania. The disorder causes people to pull out their body hair, including eyelashes.

These disorders are treated with medication and cognitive behavioral therapy. People with eating disorders such as anorexia, bulimia, and obesity have a compulsive preoccupation with food and thinness that is similar to the symptoms of OCD. A strong relationship between OCD and anorexia is suspected because many people with anorexia have clear symptoms of OCD.

People with trichotillomania compulsively pull out their body hair. Sites include the scalp, eyelashes, eyebrows, armpits, and pubic area. Stress often brings on hair pulling episodes, although for some people with TTM, hair pulling is also a problem when they are relaxed. They may pull hair while watching television.

Or they may pull at hairs while reading, for example. Self-injurious skin picking is sometimes called neurotic excoriation, dermatillomania, or self-inflicted dermatoses. People with this disorder pick at their skin to the point of damaging it. Sometimes they do this to satisfy an urge, similar to the urge people with TTM have. Others pick at their skin to make areas look smoother, more even, or just "better" in some way. People with skin-picking problems can also benefit from cognitive behavioral therapy similar to that used for trichotillomania.

Body dysmorphic disorder involves a persistent preoccupation with a minor bodily defect or an imagined defect, causing severe disruption to normal functioning. People with BDD are usually shy and have low self-esteem. Any body part can be the focus of attention, but obsessions are often related to the face. They may pick and dig at their skin. Those with a type of BDD called muscle dysmorphia worry about their bodies being too small and puny. Just as people who worry about being unattractive look just fine, those with muscle dysmorphia are often just the opposite—large and muscular. Repetitive and time-consuming behaviors such as grooming, shaving, washing, skin picking, weight lifting, appearance checking in mirrors, and comparing themselves with others are typical of BDD.

People with BDD are often unaware that their worries are excessive and unfounded. Dermatologic treatment or cosmetic surgery for perceived defects is often sought, only to have the worries return. Major depression is more prevalent in people with BDD, and they are and at higher risk of suicide than the general population. Help from a mental health professional is unlikely to be sought until depression becomes significant.

Hypochondriasis is a preoccupation with fears of having a severe medical condition. The fears persist even after being reassured by medical professionals that the person is physically healthy. People with hypochondriasis engage in compulsions that are triggered by their obsessive health concerns. Compulsions can include repeatedly checking the body for signs of disease, frequently asking doctors and loved ones for reassurance that no disease exists, and going for repeated medical consultations and tests. Some people with BDD repeatedly check the Internet for medical information (cyberchondriasis) about diseases and disorders they fear they may have.

Other disorders that are seen more frequently in people with OCD are referred to as comorbid disorders. They include depression, Tourette's syndrome, tic disorders, attention deficit disorder, oppositional defiant disorder, learning disorders, Asperger's syndrome and other anxiety disorders.

A man unintentionally swears and flails his arms at a stranger on the street. He suffers from Tourette's syndrome, characterized by vocal and physical tics. Some people with OCD also live with other neurobehavioral disorders, such as Tourette's.

Tourette's Syndrome

Tourette's syndrome is an inherited neurological disorder that affects about 200,000 people in the United States. It is characterized by repeated and involuntary body movements and vocalizations. These are called tics. Symptoms begin before the age of twenty-one and last at least one year. Boys are three to five times more likely to have Tourette's syndrome. It occurs in only one out of every two thousand children, but as many as 15 percent of children have transient tics. These are tics that come and go. In a minority of cases, the vocalizations can include socially inappropriate words and phrases. This is called coprolalia. These vocal outbursts are neither intentional nor purposeful. Tics can be described as sudden and repetitive urges to make virtually any movement or sound, including the following:

- Eye blinking
- Squinting
- Lip smacking
- Neck jerking
- Shoulder shrugging
- Arm flailing or thrusting
- Nail biting
- Foot stomping, kicking
- Jumping
- Barking
- Throat clearing
- Blowing air through the mouth
- Coughing, sniffing

- Hissing
- Humming
- Stuttering
- Sudden changes of voice tone, tempo, or volume
- Short, often meaningless phrases
- Swearing

Many children with Tourette's syndrome or tic disorders also have another neuropsychiatric disorder, such as attention deficit hyperactive disorder (ADHD) or OCD. When a child has both Tourette's syndrome and OCD, it's important to distinguish between tics and OCD symptoms because the treatments differ. Yet it can be difficult to tell if a symptom is a tic or an OCD ritual. The major difference is that a tic is preceded by a sensory feeling, whereas an OCD compulsion is preceded by a thought.

However, this clinical distinction between Tourette's syndrome and OCD has its limits. This is especially true with children who have compulsions such as counting, symmetry, repeating, and ordering that are not preceded by catastrophic ideas about harm or danger to themselves or others. This has led some clinicians to the idea that there's a form of OCD that seems to arise from a blend of OCD and Tourette's syndrome. This has been termed Tourettic OCD. In this case, compulsions are typically preceded by feelings of internal tension or a sense of generalized physical discomfort, rather than intrusive thoughts. The resulting compulsions must be performed "just right" to relieve this state of internal tension.

In light of this newly described form of OCD, parents should be alert to the need for modified, more flexible approaches to the use of medications and CBT for their children.

www.usatoday.com

USA TODAY
Life
SECTION D

January 11, 2000

From the Pages of USA TODAY

Mental misery besieges many

About 20 million Americans suffer from recurrent bouts of major depression, studies show. And although research is promising, experts still aren't sure who is vulnerable or exactly how to treat it.

"The need for research in this area is critical," says Martin Keller, a pioneering researcher at Brown University [in Rhode Island].

As mental health professionals pursue answers, the costs of major depression to sufferers and to society remain huge, Keller says. "Estimates are that the economic costs . . . in the United States are more than $53 billion a year."

And the personal risk is high: Major depressive disorders account for about 20% to 35% of suicides, says the recent study *Mental Health: A Report of the Surgeon General.*

Obviously, this is not some version of the post-holiday blues. Recurring depression means repeated plunges into an abyss [deep well of hopelessness], with profound feelings of despair and loss of interest in life, plus debilitating physical effects such as insomnia.

The causes of depression include genetic, biological, personality and environmental factors. One bout is bad enough. But without any treatment, 80% to 90% of those who suffer a single battle with serious depression will have a second attack within two years, the surgeon general's report says. Toughest of all for sufferers: Even with treatment, large numbers will have repeated episodes.

Mental health professionals and researchers emphasize there is hope. "The good news is that we have treatments that are effective in modifying long-term or major depression, prolonging recovery and maintaining wellness," says Charles Reynolds, a researcher and psychiatrist with the University of Pittsburgh School of Medicine [in Pennsylvania].

The big guns in the treatment of recurrent depression are a variety of antidepressant drugs. New ones are continually being researched. But they are not foolproof. Patients treated for a major depressive episode with medications have a 30% chance of having a second one, says Jesse Rosenthal, chief psychopharmacologist at Beth Israel Medical Center in New York.

And it takes a skilled practitioner to monitor drug use, to decide what antidepressant at what dose to be taken for how long and whether a mood stabilizer also is needed.

"Drugs will suppress the depression, but the vulnerability is still there under the surface," cautions psychiatrist Frederick Goodwin, former director of the National Institute of Mental Health.

Goodwin suggests medications be taken for a year after symptoms subside to prevent relapse, then withdrawal from the drugs should be slow. Some patients may need medication indefinitely, and it is often better to stay on it than continue to stop and start.

Goodwin, Keller and others say long-term, maintenance drug therapy might be considered with:

* A first depressive episode before age 30 or after 60.
* A family history of serious depression.
* Two episodes separated by no more than two years.
* A third episode.
* Long-lasting episodes.
* Poor control of symptoms during continued therapy.
* The presence of substance abuse or an anxiety disorder.

Instead of just relying on drugs, researchers are trying other routes to block recurrence.

Jackie Gollan, working with Neil Jacobson of the University of Washington in Seattle, found that personality factors can make a difference. In her small study of patients followed for two years after a major depressive episode, 44% battled the illness again.

Gollan's patients had been treated with cognitive behavioral therapy (CBT). CBT helps patients change negative thought patterns that contribute to depression to more positive ones. Gollan finds patients who are aggressive and those who are loners are at increased risk—traits that make getting emotional support from other people more difficult.

Many practitioners are enthusiastic about psychotherapies such as CBT that help patients learn coping skills for everyday life, part of keeping depression at bay.

The most effective treatment seems to be a combination of drugs with psychotherapy, experts say.

Researcher Ellen Frank of the University of Pittsburgh finds that medication plus psychotherapy leads to an 80% chance of staying well for three years.

Fifty percent of a subset of Frank's female patients get well on just psychotherapy. "And if therapy alone doesn't cut it, adding medication to the treatment then seems to work for about 80% of the remaining half," she says.

Keller of Brown University hopes to have funding soon for a definitive, five- to 10-year study that uses both drugs and therapy.

For now, the key for sufferers and their family members and friends, he says, is to "be tuned in to the earliest symptoms of return. The sooner you catch it, the easier it is to treat."

—Karen S. Peterson

It is quite common for children and teenagers with OCD to have more than one neurobehavioral disorder. Sometimes people with OCD will resort to abusing alcohol or illegal drugs to relieve the anxiety and distress associated with OCD. This is called a dual disorder. Treatment of OCSDs, comorbid disorders, and dual disorders is challenging to mental health professionals. Often more than one specialist is involved in the treatment plan.

DEPRESSION

Depression is common among people with OCD. At the time patients seek treatment for OCD, about one-third have depression. Over their lifetime, two-thirds of people with OCD have at least one episode of depression. The same medications that help OCD also help relieve depression. This leads us to believe that OCD and depression could share some of the same neurochemical and brain structure abnormalities.

Or perhaps, depression is a natural outgrowth of the distress of OCD. Whatever the connection, the detection and treatment of depression

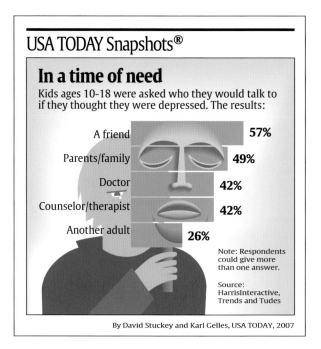

USA TODAY Snapshots®

In a time of need

Kids ages 10-18 were asked who they would talk to if they thought they were depressed. The results:

A friend — 57%
Parents/family — 49%
Doctor — 42%
Counselor/therapist — 42%
Another adult — 26%

Note: Respondents could give more than one answer.

Source: HarrisInteractive, Trends and Tudes

By David Stuckey and Karl Gelles, USA TODAY, 2007

is important. Like OCD, it is highly treatable. Symptoms of clinical depression include persistent and strong feelings of sadness, helplessness, and hopelessness; crying or frequent tearfulness; lack of energy; loss of interest in normal activities and pursuits; impaired appetite; weight loss or gain; impaired sleep; and suicidal feelings or thoughts. If you or anyone you know has any of these symptoms, it is important that you tell your parent, a doctor, or a counselor. If you or someone you know has suicidal thoughts, even occasionally, seek help now. Most cities and towns have a suicide hotline that can help you.

CHAPTER FOUR

THE IMPACT ON FAMILY AND FRIENDS

RITA'S STORY

*R*ita was thoughtful and always considering the welfare of others. *She didn't worry any more than most and did well in school. When her sister Beth was born, she rushed home from school every day, just so she could hold her and play with her. When Beth was six months old, Rita stayed home sick with a cold and sore throat. She was careful to stay away from Beth to avoid giving her the cold, but disturbing thoughts occurred to her: What if I cough too near her? How close is too close? What if I touched the kitchen counter after touching my face and then Mother touched it when she prepared the formula?*

Rita, feeling worried and fearful of being held responsible for harming her sister, begged her mother to clean the counter carefully several times a day. Rita stayed in her room most of the time to avoid contaminating her sister with her cold germs. She asked repeated questions about how germs were spread, anxiously seeking reassurance from both her parents that she hadn't given her sister her cold. "But what if I did?" she would ask. They reassured her over and over that all babies get colds, and it wouldn't hurt her. "Colds help build her immunity," they would tell her, again and again. These reassurances would help for a short while, but soon Rita's worries and distress would be back.

After she was over her cold, Rita was never so glad to go back to school. She knew she couldn't harm her sister if she wasn't home and around her so much. After several days, her worries subsided. But what if her sister got a cold from somewhere else, or what if she became sick with some other illness? To counter her fears, Rita checked on her sleeping sister to make sure she was still breathing—sometimes waking up during the night to check on her. Rita didn't hold her anymore, fearing she would drop her.

Several weeks later, Rita found a tack on the floor by the bulletin board at school. Thinking it must have fallen off the board, she picked it up and stuck it tightly into the bulletin board so it wouldn't fall out. About that time, a boy and girl sitting at desks nearby were whispering. The girl, Michele, yelled, "Ouch!" This startled Rita, and she wondered why the girl yelled. Rita sat at her desk, wondered some more, and worried. Before sticking the tack in the bulletin board, had she stuck Michele with the tack? Is that why she yelled? What if the tack were really dirty? Rita worried that she could have caused a bad infection and maybe Michele could get sick and die. All day she worried.

That evening Rita was overwhelmed with fear that she had stuck Michele with the tack, causing an infection. She hardly knew Michele, but a good friend knew her well. She called her friend and got Michele's phone number, giving a fake excuse for why she needed to reach her. Rita called Michele to ask how she was doing and how she was feeling. She didn't mention the tack. She called Michele back an hour later, and this time asked her if she had been injured at school. Rita asked her why she had yelled. They had just been kidding around. Michele sounded as if she thought Rita was acting strange.

Rita was relieved, but not for long. Maybe Michele was just covering up, and she didn't want to admit she really had been stuck by the tack. Maybe she was afraid Rita would hurt her again. Rita's mother found her crying in her room. She was worried and terribly upset, her throat felt raw and sore, and she was burning up with a fever. Rita's mother reassured her about the tack and then told her the most important thing at this time was to get to the clinic. The doctor did a throat culture, and Rita was treated for strep throat.

Again, Rita's obsessive thoughts and worries improved some, but not completely. She still checked on her sister frequently. She refused to hold her or even touch her for fear that she would harm her by dropping her or maybe bending an arm or leg too far. Rita called friends from school when she thought she might have caused some type of harm.

Her grades slipped because she spent so much time worrying and making phone calls. She had trouble concentrating when she tried to read or study. Every time Rita caught a cold or even had a sore throat, her mother noticed that her worries and checking would increase. After the illness, they would ease some but never go away. One day Rita asked her mother to put all the knives on the top shelf in the kitchen so the baby couldn't reach them. By now her sister was walking, but she couldn't reach the countertop yet. It did seem like a good idea to be prepared, though. When a few hours later, Rita asked her mom to hide the knives, her mother demanded to know why. Rita admitted she was afraid she might stab the rest of the family. She said she wanted the knives hidden so she couldn't find them. Crying hysterically, Rita told her mother how horrible thoughts kept going through her head over and over. She tried to think of other things. She tried praying. She tried saying special words over and over, but nothing worked. The thought that she might stab someone tortured her.

Rita's mother had never seen her so upset. She was also concerned because Rita had another sore throat. When she took her to the doctor, she asked him if the worries, intrusive thoughts, and checking could have anything to do with the strep throat. Yes, the doctor said, there could certainly be a connection. He explained to her and Rita about pediatric autoimmune neuropsychiatric disorder associated with streptococcal infections. Though they knew no cure was available, they were relieved to know there was a name for the intrusive thoughts and compulsive behavior—obsessive-compulsive disorder. They were also relieved that help was available—treatment that would help her break free from the thoughts that had been torturing her.

LETTING GO OF BLAME AND GUILT

Obsessive-compulsive disorder had quite a negative effect on Rita's family and her friends. This is usually the case. Parents want the very best for their children, and chronic illness threatens the goals, aspirations, and dreams they have for them. Often parents feel guilty, thinking the OCD is somehow their fault. Parents, siblings, friends, and the person with OCD need to understand that it is not anyone's fault. Once the guilt feelings are let go, everyone can work together to fight the real enemy, the OCD.

We've established that OCD is a neurobehavioral disorder with definite changes that can be seen in the brain with PET scans. Some chemical imbalance occurs, since medications that increase the serotonin availability decrease symptoms. So it would be difficult

The support of parents and siblings is vital to managing OCD.

USA TODAY

www.usatoday.com

USA TODAY
Life
SECTION D

October 20, 2008

From the Pages of USA TODAY

A boy's battle with Tourette's
James Patterson follows family's medical saga

Being little, really little, 5-years-old little, is supposed to be about playing with other kids in the backyard, watching *Sesame Street* on the couch while you eat Cheerios, and jumping on your bed in your pj's. Not the childhood Cory Friedman had.

Friedman's childhood experience with the disabling medical condition Tourette's syndrome, as well as obsessive-compulsive disorder, is the subject of best-selling novelist James Patterson's first non-fiction book, *Against Medical Advice*. The book was co-written by Patterson's good friend and former advertising colleague Hal Friedman, whose son, Cory, woke shortly before his fifth birthday with an uncontrollable urge to shake his head—an involuntary tic. *Against Medical Advice* delves into the Friedman family's 15-year journey to find an accurate diagnosis for Cory and a treatment that would do more good than harm.

It describes, from Cory's perspective as a teenager, how his tics became more severe, the rotating cast of medical experts consulted, the emotional ups-and-downs with teachers and schoolmates, and the multiple medications that were tried.

"I found the story very compelling," Patterson says. "I think an awful lot of people go through medical situations where, even if they're trying their best, they can't get to the solution."

Cory painfully relates the toll to justify blaming anyone for OCD—parents, siblings, friends, or patient—any more than we would blame others for being diabetic or having heart disease. That doesn't let everyone off the hook, however. Like diabetes and heart disease, there are treatments and lifestyle changes, such as those discussed in chapter 3, that can improve OCD symptoms and make it easier to live with.

Moreover, like diabetes and heart disease, family members and

Tourette's and OCD takes on his family, and his awareness yet inability to stop his distracting and destructive actions.

"I felt like a boy on the end of a puppeteer's string," he says in the prologue. "What made it worse was that I was also the puppeteer."

Friedman says he and wife Sophia, and daughter Jessie—Cory's greatest defenders—felt, "It was sometimes terrifying and maddening." Part of his turmoil came from not knowing whether the many drugs prescribed for Cory actually hurt or helped him.

Where the emotional wear and tear of Tourette's often tears families apart, Friedman says love and patience helped them weather Cory's medical kaleidoscope. "Many families like ours don't last, but we were just focused on keeping him going. My wife and I had many nights we just held each other and sobbed and prayed it would get better."

One of their biggest aims was to not allow Cory to be victimized by his condition. "We taught him to believe in and empower himself—not define himself by his medical issues," he says.

Michael Ullman, a professor of neuroscience at Georgetown University Medical Center [in Washington, D.C.], says one study he conducted found that people with Tourette's were faster than typically-developing children at processing grammar. "Maybe knowing their child is faster at something can help parents focus on the advantages, not just the disadvantages."

Cory says going through so many struggles has made life richer. "It builds character, makes me live life on a deeper level."

[Dr. John] Piacentini says since Cory was a child, diagnosing and treating Tourette's has improved significantly. His research, to be published within the next few months, and similar studies suggest that therapy to help change behaviors can be an effective alternative to drugs.

Now 24, Cory runs a fledgling Internet business. He sings in a band and rarely takes medicine. Maturity and the ability to better control his thought processes have helped lessen symptoms.

—*Mary Brophy Marcus*

friends can help with the treatment and lifestyle changes. No one is to blame for OCD. No one in a person's life causes OCD, but the people in a person's life can make a difference. They can help the person endure a life with OCD symptoms, with anxiety, fear, and distress. Family and friends can also help the person break free from the anxiety, fear, and distress of OCD. Let's approach this issue in a positive way. As we discuss the impact of OCD on family and friends, we'll discuss some things people can do to help a person with OCD break free.

EDUCATE ABOUT OCD

People with OCD often don't realize they have a diagnosable disorder with treatment available. They've labeled themselves as weird or strange. Perhaps others have also. Often a family member or friend is the first one to bring symptoms to the person's attention and encourage him or her to seek help. People without OCD will never fully understand the disease, but they can come close by reading as much as possible. To learn more, check out the information in the Resources section in the back of this book. Some areas have support groups available for family members. Talking with others can advance understanding.

It can be very helpful to talk to others who have experience with OCD to better understand the disorder.

Understanding Those with OCD

The lack of understanding by people who don't know someone with OCD can torment the person with OCD and family members. Instead of viewing lack of understanding as "wrong" or "bad," it is more accurate to view it as "yet to be educated."

THERE'S A PERSON IN THERE!

With education comes acceptance. When we understand a problem, we are much more likely to accept it. This does not mean we should accept it as a permanent problem that can't be helped but to accept it as something that can be dealt with. This means accepting the facts, yet changing what can be changed. It also means spending energy on effective solutions, rather than wasting energy on anger and resentment. These emotions use up valuable time and energy. There are bound to be some negative feelings, and these should be directed where they belong, at the OCD. The inevitable anger can be channeled constructively to support the patient's efforts toward overcoming OCD.

Everyone comes to acceptance at a different pace, however. Expecting every family member and friend to understand OCD is unrealistic. For a long time, there has been a widespread lack of understanding about psychiatric disorders, and this doesn't change overnight. It's best to expect and anticipate resistance to even the most qualified sources of information by at least one family member or friend.

STOP PARTICIPATING IN RITUALS

Education and acceptance unite everyone—family members, friends, and the person with OCD—as a team, joined by a goal of recovering from OCD. But perhaps the most challenging aspect of helping a child or adult with OCD involves taking a hard, honest look at how family members participate in the OCD rituals and addressing this problem head-on.

When OCD thoughts and feelings creep into a person's life, relief is sought through the carrying out of repetitive behaviors and rituals. Because OCD behaviors often do not occur in isolation, family members are drawn into the rituals in an effort to ward off the distress. The demands of the person's OCD fears upon family members are so great that to "keep the peace," family members will frequently do whatever the person demands to relieve his or her anxiety, no matter how inconvenient, repetitive, and inflexible.

USA TODAY Snapshots®

Are you fretting about messages?
How Wi-Fi users responded when asked how long they go before they get "antsy" about checking e-mail, instant messaging and social networking sites:

One hour or less
47%

One day
46%

7%
One week

Source: Impulse Research for Qwest Communications online survey of 1,063 adult Wi-Fi users in April

By Anne R. Carey and Sam Ward, USA TODAY, 2009

Finding it more disruptive to oppose her daughter's persistent demands, Rita's mother altered her family's routines "to keep the peace" despite the inconvenience to herself and other family members. Rita insisted that only plastic knives and forks be used for family meals. If the baby was sitting on a chair in the kitchen as her mother used a metal knife while cooking dinner, Rita would insist that her mother remove the baby from the kitchen as long as the knife was present. Failure to adequately warn and direct her mother would result in intense fear that she might be held responsible for any possible mishap involving the baby and the knife. Any attempt by her mother to resist Rita's demands resulted in anger and emotional outbursts.

No one is to blame for this enabling behavior, other than the disease of OCD. At first the family members don't even realize they are dealing with an illness. Switching to the use of plastic utensils may not appear like much of a sacrifice to "keep the peace." But as more and more accommodations are made to the irrational OCD fears, the disease inevitably progresses with worsening obsessions

Family members can unintentionally make accommodations for a person with OCD that can worsen the disorder. Learning to avoid certain enabling behaviors can help families better manage OCD.

and compulsions. Obsessive-compulsive disorder is never satisfied with just a few rituals or with slightly better than normal cleaning or checking. By the time the rituals get out of hand and OCD is evident, the families and sometimes friends are often fully involved.

Family members who participate in rituals are unintentionally reinforcing and strengthening OCD symptoms. Recognizing the problem is easier than doing something about it. Just stopping participation abruptly is likely to be met with anger, resentment, and increased anxiety. A better approach is to collaborate with the person who has OCD in a plan to lessen involvement with the symptoms. This is likely to occur during cognitive-behavioral therapy with an experienced therapist directing the effort. It will probably be decided to withdraw participation in rituals in steps, as part of the overall treatment. The person's therapist will advise the family on a plan of action.

Some families use self-help books to change the way they deal with OCD symptoms. We've listed books for family members and parents in the Resources section.

Everyone needs to be aware that withdrawal of participation will cause anxiety. This is hard to watch, but it's important to remember that facing the anxiety and learning more appropriate responses to it is part of recovery. When a person with OCD resists the urge to engage in rituals and feels the anxiety heighten and then decrease, new learning takes place—the rituals are not necessary. Rita's mother realized that she was doing a great deal of cleaning at her daughter's insistence, as well as accommodating Rita's fear of knives. They worked out a plan with the therapist to gradually decrease the amount of cleaning both did in Rita's effort to protect her sister from illness. As Rita made progress with her OCD, she and her mother made plans for gradually increasing the use of silverware instead of plastic utensils.

Participating in therapy sessions can help everyone in a family develop a plan to manage OCD symptoms.

WITHHOLDING REASSURANCE

Reassurance seeking is actually a compulsive behavior, a ritual. An obsessive thought occurs, causing anxiety and distress. Did I check the door? Are twenty seconds really enough time to get my hands clean enough? Could I have AIDS? After going over and over the question, people with OCD often seek reassurance from someone they trust. The answer brings immediate relief, but that relief is fleeting. The question is asked again, perhaps rephrased, or the person might ask someone else. Over time the same questions are asked over and over. The cycle of questions and reassurance becomes an ingrained family pattern that's difficult to change. Friends often become part of the pattern too.

Initially, it seems to the person with OCD and to family and friends that reassurance helps relieve the symptoms of OCD. On the contrary, it only makes them worse. Anxiety returns, and more reassurance is needed. The solution is the same as for other compulsive behaviors. The obsessive thought must be borne, and the person needs to allow the anxiety to heighten and then decrease without making the compulsive reassurance request. Those involved need to resist the urge to provide the reassurance. Avoid criticism or anger. Sometimes humor helps lighten the tension, but care must be taken that the person doesn't feel ridiculed. At first it may help to answer a question once, but only once. "I already answered that question, and I'm not supposed to repeat my answer," is a good answer to repeated questions and rephrased questions.

Some people with OCD feel a need to wash the counter multiple times a day. When the person is trying to resist the urge, using humor can sometimes make things easier.

Rita's mother, as well as her friends, discussed how they should respond to Rita's requests for reassurance. Originally the requests were constant and fraught with anxiety. They gave such answers as, "I'm not supposed to answer those kinds of questions," "It's better for your health if I don't answer that question," or "We've discussed this, and you said I'm not to answer questions like that." As treatment progressed and Rita's anxiety decreased, they could tell when humor would be appropriate. They'd give answers such as, "Yes, let's clean that counter a third time today. We need it to be sterile!" or "Yes, you probably have superpowerful germs, able to leap across rooms and cause the greatest of harm!"

BE ENCOURAGING AND SUPPORTIVE

Sometimes OCD seems to take over a person's life. When OCD interferes, family members and friends will need to decide how to respond. A gentle reminder that OCD seems to have shown up might be in order. Other times a person might want to just wait it out.

When a person has resisted OCD behavior, praise is in order. Close family members and friends may share goals and be more involved in treatment. It's important to set challenging goals, but they need to be reasonable. Family and friends can help by praising accomplishments, even ones that would seem minor, even silly, to others without OCD. Making comparisons with others who have OCD is never appropriate. Every case of OCD is different, and everyone's journey toward recovery is unique and worthy of respect.

CHALLENGES AT SCHOOL

School can be an overwhelming challenge for children and teens who have OCD. Withdrawal and compulsive behaviors can affect schoolwork and relationships with peers. Since students spend so much time at school, teachers might be the first ones to suspect a student has a problem. Teachers and friends can be important team members in a student's struggle with OCD. A teacher who sees signs of OCD in a child or teen should talk with the parents in a nonjudgmental manner and encourage them to have the child seen by a pediatrician. Let the parents and the child know that school personnel are available to help.

Children and teens who have been diagnosed with OCD and are receiving treatment may need some accommodations, especially at the beginning of treatment. For example, a student may need extra time for taking tests, or homework assignments might have to be adjusted. Teachers and parents need to work together to plan how to

Friends are important in helping people manage their OCD. Sometimes friends are the first ones to spot the disorder.

Remember the Positive

t's important to remind people with OCD of the following point: They are not their OCD. Remind them of their many other positive qualities. Enjoy activities that have nothing to do with the OCD.

adjust teaching techniques to assist in cognitive- behavioral therapy. As time goes on and the OCD improves, less accommodation will be needed. This too is part of the treatment. Teachers will want to notify parents of positive and negative changes in behavior. Teasing should never be tolerated. Consider designating a "safe" person the child can turn to when the OCD gets to be too much, someone who can empathize with the struggle. We have listed resources for school personnel in the Further Reading section of this book.

SUPPORT GROUPS

It's nice to know you're not alone. A good support group can be helpful for people with OCD and their family members. It provides education about OCD and its treatment. The International OCD Foundation(IOCDF, see the Resources section) keeps a list of support groups meeting all across the United States and in numerous countries. Even if there's not a group in your local area, you may still be able to find support on the Internet. Some websites dedicated to providing information about OCD have message boards, chat rooms, or pages dedicated to seeking information from experts.

Many Internet support groups exist for people with OCD and their families. A few years ago, there was one large group. Today there are several specialized groups for family members, parents, teens, children, and people with specific symptoms. Find a regularly updated list of online support groups at http://health.groups. yahoo.com/group/OCDSupportGroups/links. People with OCD and their families can get support and share information from others experiencing the same struggles. The original large e-mail list for the discussion of the effects of OCD and its treatment is at http:// health.groups.yahoo .com/group/OCD-Support. The site includes contributions from OCD experts.

You can join the e-mail list for teens with OCD at http://health. groups.yahoo.com/group/newocdteen. Teens with OCD and related

In support groups for people with OCD, people share information and get support.

disorders can post questions and get answers about dealing with OCD in their lives. Two OCD behavioral experts screen all posts and provide answers to questions.

The National Alliance on Mental Illness (NAMI) has discussion groups on its website at http://www.nami.org for people with OCD, family members, or anyone interested in learning more about obsessive-compulsive disorder.

CHAPTER FIVE

LIVING WITH OCD

Those diagnosed with OCD may ponder how their lives will be affected by the disorder as they grow older. For some, getting appropriate treatment early can result in a life with minimal OCD symptoms. A few will continue to have moderate to severe symptoms. However, for most, living with OCD means receiving treatment and then living with mild obsessive thoughts and compulsive behaviors that wax and wane with the stresses of life.

In 1992 a Dutch doctor, Per Hove Thomsen, followed up on forty-seven children after they had received treatment for OCD. Twenty-seven percent of the children had no OCD symptoms as adults. Twenty-six percent had mild symptoms that no longer qualified as OCD. Twenty- one percent had moderate OCD symptoms when they were under stress, but they were only mild at other times. Twenty-six percent of the children had more severe OCD throughout their lives. We expect much better results in the coming years, since today's treatments are yielding even more improvement of OCD symptoms.

The young people you've met throughout this book received cognitive-behavioral therapy to help them better manage their OCD. Let's look at some things they learned along the way.

ANGELA'S STORY

Angela worried about cheating on a test and getting caught. The thoughts of OCD tend to be ones that would be the most hurtful and worrisome to the individual. Since morality and honesty meant so much to Angela, the idea of cheating on a test was devastating. The remote possibility that she could be suspected of cheating seemed unbearable.

With every test, she took more precautions to make certain, absolutely certain, that she would not cheat and that she would not be suspected of cheating. She partially covered her paper with her hand and bent her head down low with her eyes inches from the paper. Some days she even stayed home from school to avoid taking tests.

Difficult as it was, Angela had to accept that she could indeed be suspected of cheating on a test. When she thought it through to a logical conclusion, she knew the possibility was remote. Even if she were suspected or even found guilty, the consequences wouldn't be all that severe. Thinking more logically about it helped some, but not much. The anxiety was still there. The most important part of her treatment was exposure and response prevention— taking tests, enduring the anxiety, and not engaging in her usual compulsive behaviors. At first she raised her head to 10 inches (25 cm) from her paper and then raised her head completely. Then she deliberately looked around the room during the test. The anxiety was horrible at first, but each time, it decreased faster.

Between tests, she imagined a scenario: She was taking a test in a normal fashion. At one point, her therapist had her imagine that she did cheat on a test, was taken to the principal's office, and was suspended from school. In her imaginary scenario, her parents were embarrassed and her father even lost his job. After doing this imaginal exposure and response prevention exercise many times, the anxiety left, and she even found herself laughing at the scene.

ALEX'S STORY

By the time Alex began cognitive-behavioral therapy, he was spending hours every day checking. He checked his homework to make sure he'd answered the questions correctly and written his papers neatly. He loved to play video games but had very little time to play once he had *checked all the connections and made sure all the cords were aligned perfectly. None of the cords could touch one another.*

His ERP exercises included turning on his video game player and TV, playing a game, and turning off the player and TV. Sounds simple enough, but he was not to check the connections before or after. He also crossed the cords so they were touching one another haphazardly. Homework was done without checking it afterward. Alex didn't do all this the first day. His therapist helped him list his rituals and rank each by severity. To start with, he picked ones for which stopping would cause only moderate anxiety. Gradually, he worked up to where he could switch on his video player and play a game without thinking much about the connections.

NICK'S STORY

Nick had received cognitive-behavioral therapy for OCD in grade school. The symptoms had improved so much that he'd believed he was cured. When he began to have intrusive thoughts about being gay, Nick didn't recognize them as OCD thoughts until they were out of control and causing intense anxiety. His psychiatrist recommended cognitive-behavioral therapy "booster sessions" to help him deal with these new symptoms. Nick learned that he would always have to be alert for new obsessive thoughts and compulsive behaviors. Applying the skills he had learned in therapy at the first emergence of symptoms would keep the OCD under better control.

Deep down Nick knew he wasn't homosexual. Because the thoughts that he might be gay or that others might think he was gay were bothersome to him, he had difficulty dismissing them. Meaningless thoughts sometimes annoy people with OCD, but the most troublesome are the ones that attack the very core of who a person thinks he or she is. Trying to get rid of them only makes the thoughts stronger. Nick learned to let the thoughts pass through his mind without resisting them. He observed them, noted they were there, and labeled them as OCD thoughts. Brain noise.

Nick also had to identify the many compulsive behaviors he had developed. He stopped checking his appearance in mirrors and took his hands out of his pockets when he was at school. Walking down the hall, he deliberately swung his arms at times, fighting the fear that he would reach out and grab someone. He recognized this as an OCD fear—possible but highly unlikely.

AMY'S STORY

To Amy the world was a dirty and dangerous place. Every day something more seemed contaminated until her world had narrowed to mainly her room and her desk at school. She felt compelled to wash her hands if she touched anything else. Showers lasted up to an hour. Amy missed so many days of school that she had to be tutored to keep up with her class. Medication helped reduce her obsessive thoughts about contamination and somewhat eased the urge to wash and shower.

After several weeks of medication, she was better able to participate in cognitive-behavioral therapy. She reduced the number and length of showers. Gradually, she touched more things she considered contaminated and resisted the urge to wash her hands.

Amy talked with her friends and explained why she had been avoiding them. She was surprised at how supportive they were. They encouraged her to resist washing her hands when the urge seemed intense and helped her get caught up on her schoolwork.

NATHAN'S STORY

Most people have learned to live with the fear of terrorist attacks, going on with their daily lives, only somewhat more alert to the many *threats to security. For Nathan, already gripped by obsessive fears of AIDS, anthrax became a great fear after he read how anthrax spores were used as a bioterrorism weapon in 2001. He searched the Internet and learned about many other diseases. Sure, they were all rare, but he could be the one to be infected. He had to make certain he was protected. He avoided touching the mail, washed his hands one hundred times a day, checked his body for any signs of disease, and changed his clothes as soon as he came home from school.*

With cognitive-behavioral therapy, the obsessive thoughts about catching a disease never left Nathan, although they became weaker. The less he responded to them, the weaker they became. He is working on accepting the uncertainty of living in a world where bad things happen. He is trying to live in the moment and enjoy the present, instead of letting OCD steal his joy.

RITA'S STORY

For Rita, learning to live with uncertainty was also an important part of her treatment. She couldn't prevent every bad thing from happening to her sister or to her friends. When it came to protecting those she loved from harm, obsessive-compulsive disorder had clouded the line between reasonable safety precautions and compulsive behaviors. Rita's therapist helped her and her mother decide what were appropriate precautions in a household with a small child. She learned to recognize obsessive fears and worries that she had harmed someone at school as OCD. At first it was hard, but she gradually found it easier to resist the temptation to call and check on the "offended" friend.

Knowing that strep throat was part of the problem helped Rita a great deal. She was on the lookout for any signs of infection and saw the doctor whenever she had a sore throat so she could get prompt treatment with antibiotics. When she did have strep throat and increased OCD symptoms, it wasn't so bad because she expected it, recognized it, and worked extra hard using the techniques she had learned in cognitive-behavioral therapy.

JASON'S STORY

For Jason, recognizing his many rituals was a big step toward recovery. He realized that counting, walking through doorways in a certain way, and not stepping on cracks were taking up a lot of time and interfering greatly with his life. Using exposure and response prevention methods, his therapist guided him, step-by-step, to reduce and eventually stop his rituals. The anxiety was fierce at first. Then, through repeated exposure to the anxiety-producing thoughts, the fear that something bad would happen if he didn't perform his ritual lessened. As time went on, though, he began to recognize more rituals. Some he hadn't recognized as OCD, and others he had developed to replace the ones he'd stopped. He sometimes felt like a detective, tracking down rituals and getting rid of them.

LUCY'S STORY

As time drew near for Lucy to go off to college, clearly, she would need to go through the things in her room and the many boxes she had stored in the garage. The thought of parting with any of the things she'd collected caused great anxiety. Yet she knew she couldn't continue her hoarding behavior in a college dorm. Lucy's therapist helped her understand this was OCD. Deciding what to do with an item led to obsessive contemplation. The thoughts of letting go before deciding caused anxiety. Compulsive hoarding relieved the anxiety. With her therapist, Lucy divided her things into four piles: things to keep and take to college, to store at home, to give away, and to throw away. Then

August 22, 2006

From the Pages of USA TODAY

Workplaces quit quietly ignoring mental illness; Services grow to help workers, as well as bottom line

Despite its stigma, a growing number of employers and employees are addressing a topic that has long been taboo: mental illness in the workplace. Employees' emotional health, a topic that once seemed incongruous with the survival-of-the-fittest corporate arena, is getting attention as a real bottom-line issue. Employers are beefing up mental health services as new research shows the staggering cost of mood disorders—depression, anxiety and panic disorder, bipolar disorder, schizophrenia and obsessive-compulsive disorder—can have on businesses.

For example:

*High costs. Untreated mental illness costs the USA $105 billion in lost productivity each year, with U.S. employers footing up to $44 billion of the bill, according to the National Mental Health Association, an Alexandria, Va.-based non-profit.

*Threat of litigation [legal action]. Federal guidelines issued in 1997 explain how employers can make accommodations for employees with serious mood disorders. Those who don't make accommodations, such as changing an employee's work hours, could be sued. The guidelines are further explanations of the Americans with Disabilities Act [ADA], issued by the Equal Employment Opportunity Commission [EEOC]. In fiscal 2004, the EEOC took in $469,000 in financial settlements for employees who complained that they'd been discriminated against because of their depression: 889 cases were filed. By 2005, that amount ballooned to more than $3 million, and there were 1,005 cases filed in that fiscal year.

she learned how to help determine which items to keep and which ones to get rid of.

With the help of her behavior therapist, Lucy went through the difficult process of confronting her fear of discarding items that, for

"There is a greater understanding among employers about these issues," says Chris Kuczynski, assistant legal counsel with the EEOC. Cases filed under the Disabilities Act have become easier to win as the public becomes more aware of mental health issues.

*More emphasis on employer help. A number of employers are enhancing mental health coverage or programs. The number of firms with employee-assistance programs, which often provide on-call counselors and referrals, has climbed from 68% in 2001 to 71% this year, according to the Society for Human Resource Management. Seven in 10 offer mental health insurance. Eighteen percent have grief- recovery programs, up from 12% in 2002.

In many cases, those with mood disorders qualify for employment protections under the federal Americans with Disabilities Act, which means employers must make accommodations to help with work.

In order for a mood disorder to be a disability, it must limit a major life activity, such as an employee's ability to sleep or take care of himself or herself. Some types of accommodations have included allowing employees to work from home, modifying supervisory methods, reassigning them or changing a work schedule.

But employers can ask for documentation of mental illness to be sure a disorder is legitimate, and they can argue whether that disorder is truly a disability under the ADA. Traits such as irritability or chronic lateness are considered behaviors, not mental impairments requiring accommodations. Employers don't have to make accommodations if doing so would impose an undue hardship, and they cannot retain an employee if that worker poses a direct threat.

Lucinda DuToit, director of human resources at Digineer, a technology consulting firm in Minneapolis [Minnesota], says the shift from ignoring to acknowledging mental illness has come as employers become more aware of the link between personal and professional lives.

She also says employers stand to gain valued loyalty from these workers if they make the necessary accommodations.

"There's much more of an understanding of mental illness. In the past, it was just, "We'll see you, bye,'" DuToit says. "Now it's, 'We'll get you help.'"

—Stephanie Armour

reasons even she couldn't fully understand, held excessive importance to her. Her therapist explained to her that early losses in Lucy's life (parental divorce, loneliness, and poverty) led to feelings of loss of control and powerlessness over her life. Her hoarding was, in part, *a way to gain a sense of mastery and control over objects as a way of compensating for these old feelings of powerlessness. The actual process of discarding was hard, as each item she discarded, no matter how insignificant, brought up waves of fear and emotion. Eventually, with her therapist's help, she was able to discard most of her "useless stuff" and move forward into college life.*

CARLOS'S STORY

The road to recovery Carlos needed to take might seem like a cinch to most teens, but those who are trapped by the obsessive need for neatness and order can understand how difficult it was for him. For someone who spent hours and hours in his room adjusting books on a shelf until they were "perfect," his therapist's instructions to "mess up" his room seemed impossible to do. At first he messed up his books just slightly and put his shirts on the opposite (wrong) side of his closet. Then he took some of the books off the shelves and stacked them on his bureau "incorrectly." He rearranged his socks so they were "imperfectly" stacked in his drawer. At school he made a point of arranging his

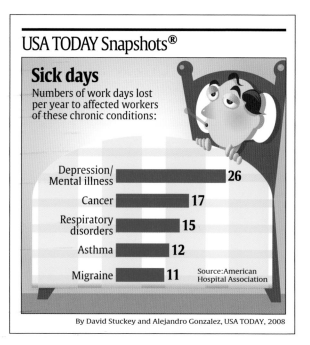

USA TODAY Snapshots®

Sick days

Numbers of work days lost per year to affected workers of these chronic conditions:

Depression/Mental illness	26
Cancer	17
Respiratory disorders	15
Asthma	12
Migraine	11

Source: American Hospital Association

By David Stuckey and Alejandro Gonzalez, USA TODAY, 2008

things on his desk differently each day.

At first the anxiety Carlos felt in his newly cluttered world seemed unbearable, but over the following days and weeks, it gradually subsided. One day his mother yelled at him for leaving laundry on the floor. He looked up, startled, because his mother never yelled. Then they both burst out laughing.

A BRIGHT FUTURE

The teens you've met in this book represent the millions of people who are living with the obsessive thoughts of OCD. Often the thoughts fade, much like noise in the distance. Rarely do the thoughts disappear entirely. However, people with OCD are realizing that they can choose to react differently to the obsessive thoughts. Medication and cognitive- behavioral therapy are allowing these choices. For some, though, even the latest treatments offer only minimal improvement. Even in these cases, there's reason for continued hope. Research and new treatments continue at a rapid pace. One day we'll better understand the many varieties of OCD and how to tailor treatments to meet the needs of people with severe cases.

GLOSSARY

antibody: a protein that is secreted into the blood or lymph in response to an antigen, such as a bacterium, virus, parasite, or transplanted organ. Antibodies neutralize antigens by binding to them.

antidepressants: medications that are designed to ease depression. Some also relieve the symptoms of OCD.

anxiety: an overwhelming sense of apprehension and fear concerning a perceived threat. It is often accompanied by physiological signs, doubt about the reality and nature of the threat, and self-doubt about one's ability to cope with the threat.

body dysmorphic disorder (BDD): a disorder in which a person has an excessive preoccupation with the appearance of a part of the body, often the face, that is perceived to be abnormal

cognitive-behavioral therapy: a psychological therapy that helps people modify behavior and change dysfunctional thinking patterns and beliefs

comorbid disorders: disorders seen together in the same patient

compulsions: repetitive behaviors or mental acts that are often performed in an effort to diminish or neutralize the anxiety and distress brought on by the obsessive thoughts of OCD

deep brain stimulation (DBS): a surgical treatment that involves sending electrical stimulation to a particular region of the brain through implanted electrodes connected to an implanted battery

depression: an emotional state characterized by symptoms such as persistent and strong feelings of sadness, helplessness, and hopelessness; crying or frequent tearfulness; lack of energy; loss of interest in normal activities and pursuits; impaired appetite; weight loss or gain; impaired sleep; and suicidal feelings or thoughts

dual disorders: disorders in which an individual is affected by both an emotional or psychiatric illness and chemical dependency

eating disorders: disorders, such as anorexia nervosa, bulimia nervosa, and binge-eating disorder, in which a person has extreme attitudes, emotions, and behaviors involving weight and food issues

exposure and response prevention: a behavioral therapy technique in which a person confronts a feared situation by doing the actions or thinking the thoughts that create discomfort or fear and at the same time try to refrain from doing the usual ritual to reduce the discomfort; also called exposure and ritual prevention

Gamma Knife: a surgical tool used for brain surgery. It acts by focusing low-dosage gamma radiation on a precise target.

monosymptomatic hypochondriasis: a disorder in which a person is preoccupied with the idea of having a severe medical condition. Worries and distress are based on the misinterpretation of bodily symptoms and persist even after seeking medical attention and receiving repeated reassurance.

neurobehavioral disorders: disorders characterized by behavioral problems that occur because of the way the brain functions

neurotransmitters: chemical substances that transmit nerve impulses across synapses in the brain. They are like chemical messengers that communicate between nerve cells.

obsessions: persistent impulses, ideas, images, or thoughts that intrude into a person's mind, often causing intense anxiety and distress

obsessive-compulsive disorder: a neurobehavioral disorder in which people have obsessions and/or compulsions that are time consuming, distressing, or interfere with normal routines, relationships with others, or daily functioning

obsessive-compulsive personality disorder: a disorder in which an excessive concern with details, rules and regulations, lists, orderliness, exactness, and being in control seriously interferes with a person's relationships or daily functioning

obsessive-compulsive spectrum disorders: disorders in which symptoms such as repetitive and intrusive thoughts play a major part. They appear to be related to OCD and include trichotillomania, body dysmorphic disorder, monosymptomatic hypochondriasis, and some eating disorders.

PANDAS (Pediatric Autoimmune Neuropsychiatric Disorders Associated with Streptococcal Infections): a psychiatric disorder, such as OCD, that is the result of the body producing antibodies against streptococci bacteria that attack certain key areas in the brain

PET (positron electron tomography) scan: a computergenerated image of biological activity in various tissues of the body

selective serotonin reuptake inhibitors (SSRIs): a group of antidepressants that increase the amount of serotonin in the brain

serotonin: a neurotransmitter that is vital to the brain's capacity to properly regulate moods. An imbalance of serotonin contributes to OCD symptoms.

trichotillomania: a disorder in which patients compulsively pull out their body hair. Sites can include the scalp, eyelashes, eyebrows, axillary area (armpit), body, and pubic area. Pulling out hair can be done deliberately or absentmindedly.

RESOURCES

Anxiety Disorders Association of America (ADAA)
8730 Georgia Ave · Silver Spring, MD 20910
240-485-1001 · www.adaa.org

This organization is dedicated to informing the public, healthcare professionals, and legislators that anxiety disorders are real, serious, and treatable. This website has information about anxiety disorders, treatment, and medications. It also offers self-tests and help finding a therapist.

Association for Behavioral and Cognitive Therapies (ABCT)
305 Seventh Ave., 16th Floor · New York, NY 10001-6008
212-647-1890 · www.abct.org

This organization is dedicated to enhancing public awareness of cognitive-behavioral therapy. The website offers good definitions of cognitive therapy, behavioral therapy, and psychotherapy; fact sheets on many diseases; trauma/disaster information; and help finding a therapist.

Cherry Pedrick's Website
www.CherryPedrick.com

Coauthor Cherry Pedrick's OCD website includes information about OCD and links to other sites with more information about the disorder.

International Foundation for Research and Education on Depression (iFred)
PO Box 17598 · Baltimore, MD 21297-1598
www.ifred.org

This organization is dedicated to researching the causes of depression, supporting those dealing with depression, and combating the stigma associated with depression. The website offers the latest information about depression, including immediate help for those considering suicide.

International OCD Foundation (IOCDF)
PO Box 961029 · Boston, MA 02196
617-973-5801 · www.ocfoundation.org

This nonprofit organization works to educate people about OCD and related disorders. It supports research into the causes and effective treatments of OCD and related disorders. Most of the books listed in our reading list are available through IOCDF. It has developed and made available *OCD in the Classroom: A Multi-Media Program for Parents, Teachers, and School Personnel.* Organized Chaos at ocfoundation.org is an excellent section on the website for teens and young adults, with articles written by teens and professionals.

Psychiatric Disability Work and School
Center for Psychiatric Rehabilitation
Sargent College of Health and Rehabilitation Sciences
940 Commonwealth Ave. W. · Boston, MA 02215
www.bu.edu/cpr/jobschool

This is a website for people with a psychiatric condition. It addresses issues and reasonable accommodations related to work and school, including information about the Americans with Disabilities Act (ADA), links to other school-and work-related sites, and advice for coping at school and work.

National Alliance on Mental Illness (NAMI)
3803 N. Fairfax Dr., Suite 100 · Arlington, VA 22203
800-950-NAMI (800-950-6264) · www.nami.org

NAMI is a national organization with affiliates in every state and more than eleven hundred communities, with the mission of support, education, advocacy, and research for people living with mental illness. The website has information on OCD and other disorders, as well as interactive bulletin boards and links to state NAMI affiliates. Also included are Child and Adolescent Action Center, Veterans Resource Center, Multicultural Action Center, and FaithNet.

National Institute of Mental Health (NIMH)
Science Writing, Press, and Dissemination Branch
6001 Executive Blvd., Room 8184, MSC 9663 · Bethesda, MD 20892-9663
866-615-6464 · www.nimh.nih.gov

The NIMH is a component of the U.S. Department of Health and Human Services. The NIMH's mission is to reduce the burden of mental illness and behavioral disorders through research on mind, brain, and behavior. The website provides access to professional journals and the latest research and statistics.

Obsessive Compulsive Anonymous (OCA)
P.O. Box 215 · New Hyde Park, New York 11040
516-739-0662 · obsessivecompulsiveanonymous.org

OCA is a twelve-step program, similar to Alcoholics Anonymous, adapted to help people with OCD. It is a fellowship of people who share their experience, strength, and hope with one another that they may solve their common problem and help others to recover from OCD. The website offers resources and information about national and international meetings.

OCD Action (OA)
Davina House, Suite 506–509 Davina House· 137–149 Goswell Rd. · London,
England EC1V 7ET
Phone: 020 7253 5272 · www.ocdaction.org.uk

This British national organization for people with OCD contains extensive information about OCD and maintains a list of independent self-help and support groups in
the United Kingdom.

OCD Resource Center of Florida
www.ocdhope.com

Coauthor Dr. Bruce Hyman's website includes information for children, teens, and
parents about OCD.

Scrupulous Anonymous
Liguori Publications · One Liguori Dr. · Liguori, MO 63057-9999
800-325-9521 · http://mission.liguori.org/newsletters/scrupanon.htm

This organization's mission is to minister to those afflicted with scrupulosity, a religious form of OCD. The website contains helpful advice for those with scrupulosity,
including the monthly Scrupulous Anonymous newsletter.

SOURCE NOTES

27–28   James Boswell, The Life of Samuel Johnson (1791; repr., New York: Penguin
        Books, 1986), 254.

   29   *Diagnostic and Statistical Manual of Mental Disorders, 4th ed., text revision*
        (Washington, DC: American Psychiatric Association, 2000), 256-257.

SELECTED BIBLIOGRAPHY

Boswell, James. *The Life of Samuel Johnson*. 1791. Reprint, New York: Penguin Books, 1986.

Diagnostic and Statistical Manual of Mental Disorders. 4th ed, text revision. Washington, DC: American Psychiatric Association, 2000.

Hyman, Bruce, Ph.D., and Cherry Pedrick, RN. *The OCD Workbook*, 3rd ed. Oakland, CA: New Harbinger Publications, 2010.

Thomsen, Per Hove. *From Thoughts to Obsessions: Obsessive Compulsive Disorder in Children and Adolescents*. London: Jessica Kingsley Publishers, 1999.

FURTHER READING AND WEBSITES

For Young Readers and Teens

Huebner, Dawn. *What to Do When Your Brain Gets Stuck: A Kid's Guide to Overcoming OCD*. What-to-Do Guides for Kids series. Washington, DC: Magination Press, 2007.

March, John S. *Talking Back to OCD: The Program That Helps Kids and Teens Say "No Way"—and Parents Say "Way to Go."* New York: Guilford Press, 2007.

Niner, Holly L. *Mr. Worry: A Story about OCD*. Morton Grove, IL: Albert Whitman and Company, 2004.

Talley, Leslie. *A Thought Is Just a Thought: A Story of Living with OCD*. New York: Lantern Books, 2004.

Wagner, Aureen Pinto. *Up and Down the Worry Hill*. 2nd ed. Rochester, NY: Lighthouse Press, 2004.

For Older Teens and Adults

Baer, Lee. *Getting Control: Overcoming Your Obsessions and Compulsions*. Rev. ed. New York: Plume, 2001.

———. *The Imp of the Mind: Exploring the Silent Epidemic of Obsessive Bad Thoughts*. New York: E. P. Dutton, 2002.

Bell, J., and M. Jenike. *When in Doubt, Make Belief: An OCD-Inspired Approach to Living with Uncertainty*. Novato, CA: New World Library, 2009.

Ciarrocchi, Joseph W. *The Doubting Disease: Help for Scrupulosity and Religious Compulsions*. Mahwah, NJ: Paulist Press, 1995.

Crawford, Mark E. *The Obsessive-Compulsive Trap: Real Help for a Real Disorder*. Rev. ed. Ventura, CA: Regal Books, 2004.

De Silva, P., and S. Rachman. *Obsessive-Compulsive Disorder: The Facts*. New York: Oxford University Press, 2009.

Foa, Edna B., and Reid Wilson. *Stop Obsessing! How to Overcome Your Obsessions and Compulsions*. New York: Bantam Books, 2001.

Grayson, Jonathan. *Freedom from Obsessive-Compulsive Disorder: A Personalized Recovery Program for Living with Uncertainty*. New York: Berkley Books, 2004.

Harrar, George. *Not As Crazy As I Seem*. New York: Graphia, 2004.

Hesser, T. Spencer. *Kissing Door Knobs*. New York: Laurel Leaf Books, 1999.

Hyman, Bruce, and T. DuFrene. *Coping with OCD-Practical Strategies for Living Well with OCD*. Oakland, CA: New Harbinger Publications. 2008.

Hyman, Bruce M., and Cherry Pedrick. *The OCD Workbook: Your Guide to Breaking Free from Obsessive-Compulsive Disorder*. 3rd ed. Oakland: New Harbinger Publications, 2010 .

Munford, P. R. *Overcoming Compulsive Checking: Free Your Mind from OCD*. Oakland, CA: New Harbinger Publications, 2004.

Murphy, T. W., M. A. Jenike, and E. E. Zine. *Life in Rewind: The Story of a Young Courageous Man Who Persevered Over OCD and the Harvard Doctor Who Broke All the Rules to Help Him*. New York: HarperCollins, 2009.

Osborn, I. *Can Christianity Cure Obsessive-Compulsive Disorder? A Psychiatrist Explores the Role of Faith in Treatment*. Grand Rapids, MI: Baker Academic and Brazos Press, 2008.

Penzel, Fred. *Obsessive Compulsive Disorders: A Complete Guide to Getting Well and Staying Well*. New York: Oxford University Press, 2000.

Tolin, D., R. Frost, and G. S. Steketee. *Buried in Treasures: Help for Compulsive Acquiring, Saving, and Hoarding*. New York: Oxford University Press, 2007.

For Parents and Family Members

Chansky, Tamar E. *Freeing Your Child from Obsessive-Compulsive Disorder: A Powerful, Practical Program for Parents of Children and Adolescents*. New York: Three Rivers Press, 2001.

Fitzgibbons, Lee, and Cherry Pedrick. *Helping Your Child with OCD: A Workbook for Parents of Children with Obsessive-Compulsive Disorder*. Oakland, CA: New Harbinger Publications, 2003.

Landsman, Karen J., Kathleen M. Rupertus, and Cherry Pedrick. *Loving Someone with OCD: Help for You and Your Family*. Oakland, CA: New Harbinger Publications, 2005.

March, John S. *Talking Back to OCD: The Program That Helps Kids and Teens Say "No Way"—and Parents Say "Way to Go."* New York: Guilford Press, 2006.

Wagner, Aureen Pinto. *What to Do When Your Child Has Obsessive-Compulsive Disorder: Strategies and Solutions*. New York: Lighthouse Press, 2002.

For Teachers

Adams, Gail B., and Marcia Torchia. *School Personnel: A Critical Link in the Identification, Treatment, and Management of OCD in Children and Adolescents*. Milford, CT: Obsessive-Compulsive Foundation, 1998.

Cooley, Myles L. *Teaching Kids with Mental Health and Learning Disorders in the Regular Classroom: How to Recognize, Understand, and Help Challenged (And Challenging) Students Succeed*. Minneapolis: Free Spirit Publishing, 2007.

Dornbush, Marilyn, and Sheryl Pruitt. *Teaching the Tiger: A Handbook for Individuals Involved in the Education of Students with Attention Deficit Disorders, Tourette Syndrome or Obsessive-Compulsive Disorder*. Duarte, CA: Hope Press, 1995.

WEBSITES

Depression and Bipolar Support Alliance
www.dbsalliance.org

This website is filled with information about depression and bipolar disorder. You'll also find depression and anxiety screening, support for loved ones, and discussion forums.

National Tourette Syndrome Association
www.tsa-usa.org

This organization offers resources for people with Tourette's syndrome (TS). Part of the web site is dedicated to young people with TS. In addition to information for children and teens with TS, it also has material that can help educate friends and classmates about TS.

LERNER

SOURCE™

Expand learning beyond the printed book. Download free, complementary educational resources for this book from our website, www.lerneresource.com

INDEX

ABOUT THE AUTHORS

Bruce M. Hyman, Ph.D., LCSW, is in private practice in Hollywood-Fort Lauderdale, Florida, and is the director of the OCD Resource Center of Florida. He specializes in the treatment of adults and children with OCD and other anxiety disorders.

Cherry Pedrick, R.N., is a registered nurse and a freelance writer living in Lacey, Washington.

PHOTO ACKNOWLEDGMENTS